D1162441

ROSS PETERSON

Books by Allen Spraggett

ROSS PETERSON

NEW WORLDS OF THE UNEXPLAINED

THE CASE FOR IMMORTALITY

THE WORLD OF THE UNEXPLAINED

KATHRYN KUHLMAN:
    THE WOMAN WHO BELIEVES IN MIRACLES

PROBING THE UNEXPLAINED

THE BISHOP PIKE STORY

THE UNEXPLAINED

ROSS PETERSON

The New Edgar Cayce

BY ALLEN SPRAGGETT
Foreword by F. Logan Stanfield, M.D.

1977
DOUBLEDAY & COMPANY, INC., GARDEN CITY, NEW YORK

The photographs of the Allen Spraggett-Ross Peterson November 1974 videotape interview, part of Mr. Spraggett's television series: "ESP—Extra-Special People," are used with the kind permission of the Global Television Network (Canada), on which the program was first broadcast.

ISBN 0-385-12298-5
Library of Congress Catalog Card Number 76–44054

For my daughter, Alanna, who, though named after me, is very much her own person—an individualist *de luxe*. Long may she continue to be . . .

FOREWORD

by F. Logan Stanfield,
B.S. in M.E., M.M.E., M.D.

As a psychiatrist and a psychoanalyst, I am naturally interested in anything which sheds new light on the vast
mystery of the human mind.

This noteworthy book goes a long way indeed toward
elucidating the mind's hidden paranormal powers and,
more important, just *how* these powers can be made
manifest at will.

Ross Peterson, the subject of this impressively documented account, is an unusual man. But he is unusual,
I'm convinced from my personal studies of him, not because he possesses unique gifts but because he has

learned how to develop potentialities which many, if not all of us, have.

To me, the major significance of this startling book is its clear implication that psychic functioning—in the sense of consistent demonstration of ESP—is essentially a normal human skill which, like any other skill, can be acquired by proper motivation, training and diligence.

I commend this book, as a faithful record of one man's remarkable trailblazing psychic achievement, to all those who believe with me in the unlimited potential of human beings.

CONTENTS

OVERTURE

All things are forgiven of him
who has perfect candor.

Walt Whitman

This is the most candid biography of a living psychic ever
written.

When I first laid eyes on Ross Peterson, the subject of
this book (who had been described to me as no less than
"a second Edgar Cayce"), there was an immediate gut reaction.

I distrusted him intensely.

In fact, I cracked to my companion: "Bet the guy's had
six wives and been in jail."

As it turned out, I was right. On both counts.

Peterson, I later learned, was then on his sixth wife
(subsequently he took a seventh) and had graced more

than one jail cell, mainly, it seems, for minor escapades arising from difficuties with one of his sundry spouses.

Yes, I admit that on that first meeting, even before speaking with the man, I prejudged him. And his alleged psychic powers.

"Psychic?" I snorted. "He's about as psychic as a duck-billed platypus!"

However, I have had to eat those words, and that is why this book is being written.

It is the recantation of a former heretic.

Ross Peterson has proved to be possibly the most remarkable trance clairvoyant in the world today.

Seasoned aficionado that I am of psychics, seers, sensitives, teacup and Tarot card readers, astrologers, and other practitioners of divination, even I admit astonishment at the range of his paranormal powers.

However, it was only after an entire year spent checking and double-checking his claimed psychic abilities that I was finally dragged, kicking and screaming, into the ranks of the converted.

As the biography of a contemporary psychic this has at least one notable difference from others of its genre: It does not glorify the subject. Nor does he want to be glorified.

Like Cromwell (or was it Lincoln?) he said: "Leave the warts in."

Ross Peterson does not purport to be anybody's conception of a stained-glass saint. Unlike the late Bishop James A. Pike, whose posthumous biography revealed that his private life, riddled with sex, scandal, deceit and drunkenness, was a flagrant contradiction of his public image, Peterson has no desire to appear to be other than what he is.

"As they say, let it all hang out," he told me when we discussed how this book was to be written.

Peterson does not aspire to be another guru, white-

robed or otherwise, preaching instant enlightenment to
those who worship him. Nor does he claim a copyright on
revelations from on high. Neither does he pretend, pope-
like, to any quasi-infallibility in his psychic readings.

"Each reading," he says, "must stand on its own feet. It
must be checked out. The overwhelming majority of them
prove to be true and helpful to the person for whom
they're given. But I claim no blanket inerrancy for anything I say, in trance or out of it."

Ross Peterson is first and last a human being. He is of
the earth, earthy. He can be exasperatingly rude and
crude at times, and at other times movingly kind and
compassionate.

After a very stormy voyage through the seas of matri-
mony, holy and unholy, he believes he has found true harmony at last with his seventh wife, Irva, but he has no
desire to conceal the erratic course by which he arrived at
his present peace of mind. (And I believe he has found
genuine peace of mind.)

Along with inner peace he has learned, at great cost in
self-discipline, how to tap a Source of psychic knowledge
so gigantic, so encompassing, so virtually universal in its
scope, that I think it can justly be compared to that of the
late, great Edgar Cayce.

In a sentence: Ross Peterson, over the forty-seven years
of his life, has evolved, through painful struggle, from a
moral and spiritual vagrant into one of the psychic gen-
iuses of our time.

He performs feats which are not only astounding but,
unlike such psychic grandstanding as mentally bending
spoons and keys, bring tangible help to people in need.

Along with his psychic powers, Ross has developed a
rare wisdom, a compassion, an understanding of the
human condition and a love for his fellowman which,
though bearing little overt resemblance to traditional
sanctimonious piety (he can still curse like the truck

driver he once was), emanates from him as a sort of benign radiation. That is, when you get to know him.

At first glance he still strikes some people as looking "cadaverous" (as one man put it). No doubt his long siege of alcoholism, of which he speaks frankly in this book, ravaged his health. Yet in the three years I have known him a steady physical, as well as moral, regeneration seems to be taking place.

The story of this incredible transformation of a spiritual bum into one of the most gifted and devoted psychics of our time is what this book is about.

I believe Ross Peterson's saga of self-defeat turned into victory is remarkable and inspiring. As he says: "If *I* could make it; if *I* could develop my psychic and spiritual perceptions to the point I have—well, *anybody* can do it."

And that could mean you, dear reader . . .

Chapter One

TESTED ON TELEVISION

It was November 1974 and Ross Peterson was a guest on my weekly program, "ESP—Extra-Special People," on Canada's Global Television Network.

At this point in time, I had known Peterson for about a year. From an initial profound skepticism, and even dislike, of the man I had come to suspect (mind you, merely *suspect*) that he did have something after all.

At my first meeting with him, a year earlier, though he must have sensed my hostility, he gave me a trance minireading which included the strikingly apposite observation that I had four calcium stones in my left kidney.

This took me a trifle aback since X-rays had just revealed the presence of four stones in my left kidney. However, I quickly recovered my skepticism and said to myself: "Could have been a lucky guess—a helluva lucky one, to be sure, but quite possible. After all, many men in their early forties have kidney stones, and as for picking the correct kidney, the left one, he had a fifty-fifty chance. And the number of the stones, four? Well, that was sheer coincidence."

No, the kidney stones, though superficially impressive, did not convince me that Ross Peterson was genuinely psychic.

Furthermore, I didn't rule out the possibility that he had done prior research on me (unlikely as it seemed), and had somehow dug up facts from my medical history. As the co-author of a book on the methods of fraudulent mediums (*The Psychic Mafia*, St. Martin's Press, New York, 1976) I knew how resourceful and cunning such people can be in ferreting out obscure information about sitters they want to impress.

But in that first sitting Peterson told me something else which, though not impressive at the time, shook me up four months later. It was more significant than the hit about my kidney stones because prior research was absolutely ruled out since the event concerned lay in the future.

I gave Peterson the name of an acquaintance of mine, a newspaperman, and asked for a health check on him.

"This entity has rampant malignancy of the lower digestive tract and will leave the earth plane within the cycle of four moons."

The death sentence was as flat and unequivocal as that. The cycle of four moons I took to be Peterson's rhetorical term for four months.

The description impressed me but slightly. True, my

acquaintance had just had an operation for cancer but the malignancy, a small one, had been in his esophagus, not his lower digestive tract, and the doctors had assured him that he was now "just fine." The prospect of his dying in four months seemed infinitely unlikely.

The fact that Peterson had correctly mentioned cancer I dismissed as another coincidence. After all, the disease unfortunately is not all that rare.

However, I was admittedly more impressed when four months later my acquaintance died. Cause of death: Cancer of the colon, or lower digestive tract.

Another lucky guess on Peterson's part?

Well, I reasoned stubbornly, it *could* have been. On the other hand, I couldn't help being somewhat taken with the exactness of the coincidence.

Did Peterson have some psychic power, though probably minimal and fleeting? That seemed to me now a possibility.

This possibility was weakened, however, when two subsequent readings by Peterson yielded no verifiably accurate information about either of the individuals whose names I gave him. Once more I was prepared to write him off as a charlatan, or at best, a psychic with very modest and unpredictable gifts. Either way, I wasn't interested in pursuing any further investigation of him.

And yet, over the next year, I kept meeting people who told me that Peterson had been amazingly accurate in diagnosing their diseases and often in prescribing remedies. Some of these reports sounded impressive.

Finally, I decided to settle definitively the question of Peterson's alleged Caycelike powers. We would do it on my television program. Peterson would be brought together with a physician. The physician would provide the name of a patient known *only* to him. Peterson would go into trance, be given the name of the mystery patient and attempt to diagnose his or her condition.

Peterson readily agreed to the terms of the test. The physician we chose was Dr. F. Logan Stanfield, a psychiatrist and psychoanalyst with an interest in psychic phenomena. He picked at random the name of one of his patients and came to the television studio prepared to assess Peterson's clairvoyant description of this patient's ills.

For me, this was the crucial experiment. If Peterson passed this test, I was prepared to admit that those who were hailing him as a second Edgar Cayce might not be so naïve as I had maintained.

The program, which was videotaped, began with my briefly interviewing Ross Peterson and discussing his alleged powers. Here is part of the transcript of that section of the program.

Spraggett: Ross, in conversation I have overheard you compared to the late, great Edgar Cayce. Do you, like him, put yourself into a trance and diagnose the illnesses of people you've never seen?

Peterson: That's one of the areas we work in. However, I can honestly say about Mr. Cayce that he has to be considered a master and I'm pretty much a neophyte.

Spraggett: Well, could we say that *his* psychic feats were meticulously documented because they extended over a period of years, while yours are being studied in, what, the early exploratory stages?

Peterson: We've begun the documentation of my readings and we want the substantiation of them when they're right but also we want to know when they're wrong. We're as interested in inaccuracies as accuracies.

Spraggett: Well, on this program we have a physician who has brought the name of a patient unknown to you and later he will give this person's name to you while you're in trance and we'll find out how accurate your reading is. But first, tell us what you do when you go into the trance state. How does it happen?

Peterson: I was a professional hypnotist with my own clinic in Michigan for a number of years and going into trance is basically a state of deep hypnosis. You can call it deep meditation if you prefer. You can put any kind of label on it.

It took me about four years to develop self-hypnosis to the point where I let go completely and became totally unconscious in the trance state.

Spraggett: Who or what is the personality which claims to speak through you when you're in trance?

Peterson: My own higher self. I'm very averse to what many mediums do—that is, let some supposed spirit take over my body, whether it be an Indian chief, an Egyptian priest or some other alleged wise one. I don't discount that this works very well for some psychics.

However, I may have a vanity problem but if I want some answers I'd rather go to the top than communicate with underlings. And that's where I believe I go when I'm in trance. To the *top*.

At this point the program was interrupted by a commercial and during the break, Ross Peterson began his trance self-induction, aided and abetted by his "conductor," Irva David (later Irva Peterson, Ross's seventh wife). The conductor begins the session by asking Peterson to relax, to clear his mind, and then she offers a prayer for protection from any negative forces, whatever the source.

When the program resumed after the commercial break, the viewers saw Ross stretched out on a couch, his eyes closed, and his breathing very deep and rhythmical.

I introduced Dr. Stanfield and told the viewing audience that he had given the name and address of the mystery patient to Irva David, who would read it to Peterson once he was in trance. For reasons of "medical confidentiality," I explained, the name of the patient would be bleeped out for the viewing audience.

When Peterson seemed to have reached a satisfactory trance level (judged largely on the basis of rapid eye movements; in trance, his eyes dart continually back and forth under their closed lids, like those of a person who's dreaming) Irva, the conductor, gave him the following directions:

"Would you please allow your mind to go to whom, to where, to what, and to when it is directed. Would you please locate the form of Mrs. X, who lives at such-and-such an address, and notify us when you have located the same."

There was a pause of one minute. Then an eerie, hollow voice intoned: "Yes, we have the form."

"Would you please go over her physical form," directed Irva, "examine it thoroughly, and give any disease conditions you find, giving causes and treatments which would be helpful."

What followed, uttered in Peterson's flat, computerlike trance voice, was in substance this diagnosis:

"You will find in this entity, at the base of the cranium, on the left-hand side looking at the rear of the head, a degenerative process taking place that is organic in nature.

"There is a deterioration of tissue here, of the very brain itself, see? It causes this one to appear demented, despondent at times . . .

"This body is gravely ill . . .

"You will find a deterioration of the sheath that surrounds the whole spine, causing at this time a modest lack of co-ordination in movement, in the rhythmic flow of the body. The very nerves are deteriorating . . .

"There are lesions upon the pituitary which would cause symptoms that would be considered mental, though they are organic in nature. No organ is an island unto itself and the whole system, the whole body, has been profoundly disrupted here . . .

"That which first must be changed is in the mind of this one. Whether she realizes it or not, that which is called sickness is first manifested in the mind as sin. And the sin which this one has committed is condemnation, condemnation, condemnation. Condemnation of herself but especially of those of the opposite sex. The male. And any who would condemn, condemn, condemn, whether herself or others, not realizing that each person is unique and yet all are part of the Whole, must suffer sickness. The mental attitude must be changed first."

Peterson then went on to prescribe a variety of palliative treatments: massage of the lower back, blue light therapy, osteopathic or chiropractic adjustment of spinal misalignments (which he described in great detail), and the application of heat and castor oil packs to the kidney area to improve the elimination of toxins. (Castor oil packs were a favorite remedy of Edgar Cayce, who also placed great emphasis on subluxations, or spinal displacements, as a basic factor in disease.)

At the conclusion of the reading, Irva, the conductor, quietly instructed: "Please remove all negative influences from this entity now."

After a pause, Peterson said: "It is done."

"Allow the body to become completely relaxed," Irva instructed, "and allow any healing that is to take place to take place now."

"Done," came the response from Peterson.

"Please awaken now feeling completely refreshed and relaxed," Irva concluded.

Peterson stretched, yawned, scratched his chin, and

then opened his eyes and in a sleepy voice inquired: "Well, did you get your questions answered?"

Throughout Peterson's performance I had kept glancing at Dr. Stanfield, trying to discern from his reactions whether the psychic diagnosis was accurate or rubbish. But his face was inscrutable.

"We're going to take another commercial break," I told the viewers, "and when we return we will ask Dr. Logan Stanfield for his medical evaluation of this clairvoyant diagnosis."

Frankly, I thought he was going to pronounce the diagnosis utterly wrong. Oh well, I consoled myself, did I really expect Peterson to be able to do it? It'll make an interesting show anyway. We've exposed a fake for what he is.

However, when the program resumed and I asked Dr. Stanfield how he assessed Peterson's reading, he astounded me by saying: "His diagnosis was very highly accurate, amazingly so.

"Actually, this patient is suffering from a disease known as Huntington's chorea. This is one of the few genetically transmitted diseases, transmitted by a rare autosomal, dominant gene, and is characterized by actual *organic* changes in the brain in contrast to functional changes.

"This patient is indeed depressed, as Ross said, and is showing choreic movements. I noted with interest that Ross spoke of inco-ordinate movements to a modest degree, which this patient is actually beginning to experience at this time.

"I am very impressed by Ross staying mainly within the central nervous system, where there is actual organic damage taking place as he said."

At this point, still the devil's advocate, I interjected: "Let me put this question to you. Ross Peterson did his diagnosis blind. Is it conceivable to you that he made these hits merely by wildly lucky guessing?"

Dr. Stanfield looked amused and waited a moment before replying.

"No," he said quietly, "I'm sure there's much more than that involved. Exactly why or how Ross has this particular ability—which, incidentally, I think many people have potentially and can develop with the proper training—I'm quite amazed at his uniqueness in the degree to which he has developed his gift.

"The personality characteristics of the patient which he described were quite fascinating to me. Ross spoke of a very condemnatory attitude on her part, especially toward men, the male sex.

"Actually, at this time this patient is the victim of a delusional system in which there is a preoccupation with sexual and aggressive impulses, and feelings of persecution. The entire content of her thinking is very morbid and full of self-condemnation.

"Ross said that the patient was very hostile toward men as a whole and this is definitely true. This attitude was preceded by a number of traumatic events in her life which quite possibly led to her present state of mind.

"The reading impressed me very deeply. Its accuracy on the whole was remarkable. It's difficult to conceptualize just how such a power as this can exist but clearly it does and we have just witnessed a demonstration of it," the psychoanalyst concluded.

Well. Was I surprised! Peterson had actually done it.

It was at that moment, I think, that the thought of this book first crossed my mind . . .

Chapter Two

THE UNLIKELY SEER

Ten years ago a less likely candidate for seership than Ross Peterson would have been hard to find.

The event that changed his aimless, drifting existence and ultimately led to his developing extraordinary psychic gifts was simple enough.

He fell off a truck.

In the fall he injured his back. For help he sought out an osteopath. Besides being an adept spinal manipulator, this osteopath was an accomplished hypnotist. He used hypnosis on Peterson to deaden the pain of his back injury.

Hypnosis, the magic sleep in which the mind vanquishes the pains of the body and asserts its dominance over mere matter, was for Ross Peterson the falling apple that led to an earthshaking discovery.

The discovery was that he had, within himself, a potential power to change not only physical conditions but his personality, his character, his whole life.

A second discovery he made, equally important, was that under hypnosis he somehow knew things he had no business knowing.

For example, once during a hypnotic trance induced by the osteopath, Peterson scared the poor man out of his wits by accurately describing a violent fight he had had with his wife that very morning over another man. And Peterson described the other man in great detail.

The osteopath was terrified. He had created a monster! How could this patient, under hypnosis, reach into his mind and pluck out facts he could not possibly know?

For himself, Peterson wasn't terrified in the least by his strange experience. He was intrigued by it, fascinated by the possibilities it suggested.

If he could bring such furtive flashes of psychic vision under control, would he then be able to use ESP whenever he wanted?

And to what uses could he put it? Discovering gold or oil? Tracking missing persons? Would he go on the stage and become the greatest mind reader of all time—a *real* one?

Then, providentially, it would seem, Ross Peterson was given a book to read by a friend. It was Thomas Sugrue's *There Is a River*, the biography of America's great sleeping prophet, Edgar Cayce.

Peterson, who had never heard of Cayce before, was enchanted by the book. And from it he caught a vision.

Could he even dream that he might develop psychic powers like Cayce's? Did he have the potential for diag-

nosing illnesses and prescribing remedies even when orthodox medicine had failed?

The very thought of being able to help people in this
way, of treading in Cayce's venerable tracks, was the
most exhilarating experience Ross Peterson had ever had.

To understand what Peterson became after this crucial
turning point in his life, and exactly *how* he did it, one
must first understand and appreciate what he had been,
the road he had traveled.

So flashback . . . to childhood.

"I was born in Flint, Michigan," Ross Peterson said as
we chatted one day and he reminisced into my tape recorder.

"My father was forced by circumstances into a job that
he always felt was beneath him. Yet he did the job and
did a helluva good job at that!

"Perhaps partly to compensate for his sense of inferiority about his work my father was a tyrant at home. A
loving one, but a tyrant. He had to be boss.

"Up until the eighth grade in school I did my best to
excel, to please my father. And I did so. I was an honors
student. Then the rebel in me started to come out during
adolescence. I barely graduated from high school.

"I was very rebellious. I needed just two things to make
my world go round—booze and girls. But not in that
order. Girls always came first.

"I had my first sexual experience at the age of twelve
with a girl who was a little older than me. We did it in a
tree house out behind our home. I must say I was more
agile then than I am now.

"My sexual education continued when as a young man
of fifteen I drove a truck delivering ice in the whorehouse
district in Flint, Michigan.

"I was fanatically jealous and possessive about my girl
friends and a terrible liar too. I went steady with three or
four girls at the same time. As long as they lived on

different sides of the city or in different towns I managed to keep them all on the string.

"My marital history started when I joined the Army just after the Second World War and spent two years in Japan. I had a problem with a Japanese girl because I liked her very much and wanted to sleep with her and she had more moral fiber than I had. She wouldn't sleep with me unless I married her. She wanted to get married in a Shinto rite.

"I told her that wouldn't be recognized by the American authorities but she said she didn't care. So I said O.K., we'll get married. But remember, when the time comes to go back home to the States, I'm going.

"I left her financially well set up because I was in special services in the Army and had plenty of time to actively engage in different aspects of the black market. Yes, I left her very well off. Anyway, that was my first marriage, or quasi-marriage.

"I came back to the States and took advantage of the GI Bill of Rights to go to college. But again, my sex drive being so much stronger than anything else, about the only course I could pass in college was intercourse. That's all I was interested in.

"I met a young Jewish girl from Detroit and I was madly enamored of her and she married me—out of pity, I think, because I was so hung up on her.

"She got pregnant and we had a baby.

"The marriage only lasted a little over a year. Then my wife woke up to the fact that she had married me out of misplaced sympathy rather than love and she left to stay with a friend in New York for a trial separation. She never came back. We were divorced. That was marriage number two.

"I kept the baby, a son, and raised him, and Brit is now a Michigan state policeman, happily married and with a young son of his own. So I'm now a grandfather.

"It took about a year for my divorce to come through, so my third marital venture started about a year and a day after my second wife left me.

"I call my third wife the dingy Belgian. I met her in a bar in Owosso, Michigan. I was in the first stages of alcoholism at the time and living with my parents, who were helping me care for my son.

"The dingy Belgian satisfied something in me. The biggest problem in my life was women and she had a touch of nymphomania. Well, if you're a jealous, possessive man, as I was, I honestly believe you can only be married to a woman who will eventually enable you to satisfy your possessiveness and jealousy.

"You get what you deserve, in short. And in my case I really got what I deserved.

"My third wife was, shall we say, highly flirtatious and by actual count I ended up in court twenty-seven times, usually on assault and battery charges when she provoked me into attacking some guy she was giving the eye in a bar.

"The thirteen years that marriage lasted were either heaven or hell, never any in-between.

"My wife and I were both full-blown alcoholics and between us we drank an average of two bottles of whiskey a day. Because of my drinking, I lost a trucking business I'd managed to build up into a good thing.

"The alcoholism got so bad that on my modest income I couldn't afford to pay for the habit, so we started making our own stuff. I made a still and produced a very potent brew . . . two hundred proof!

"If you take one pound of yeast and one pillowsack full of corn or other grain, forty pounds of sugar, and you mix it in a fifty-five-gallon barrel, it will produce alcohol. Then you heat the stuff at three to five pounds pressure in a pressure cooker at a temperature of about 202 to 208 degrees and what you get is *pure* alcohol.

"The first batch I made was in a little shed behind our house. I took a fruit jar full of it—it was hotter than hell in my hands—and ran into the house and set it down on the kitchen table and called my wife, telling her the magic elixir was ready and she could test it. We had plenty of frozen orange juice in the house for a mixer.

"Then I went back to my still and spent an hour or so there gleefully adding up how many fruit jars of brew this batch would fill. When I returned to the house I couldn't find my wife but I noticed that the fruit jar on the kitchen table was half empty.

"Then I found my wife. She was lying in the corner of the living room, unconscious. The stuff was that potent!

"Now, this was about four in the afternoon. I tried to awaken her but I couldn't. I was afraid to call a doctor because he'd know why she was out cold and probably report me to the authorities for running an illicit distillery and my wife and I would both go to jail.

"Well, I spent a worrisome night. But about noon the next day my wife began to show signs of life and came out of it.

"We merrily made whiskey ever after that but we didn't drink nearly so much. A little of our brew went a long way.

"The marriage came to an end when I left my wife and told her I was going to file for divorce because we just couldn't live together in any sort of harmony. However, before the divorce proceedings started she drowned in a bathtub. I got word that while alone in the house—I had by this time moved back with my parents in another town —she apparently was preparing to take a bath, was more drunk than she realized and fell, knocking herself uncon- scious and drowning in the bath water.

"Well, in spite of the fact that I was preparing to di- vorce her, my wife's death shocked me and I felt over- whelmed, strangely enough, by a sense of loneliness. This is probably why I began my fourth marital experience about two months after my wife died.

"I found a grass widow with five children, and I had always wanted a large family, so I married her and the five kids and we all moved into a house in the boondocks of Michigan. I made my living collecting and selling junk.

"Frankly, that part of it, the junk dealing, was a lot of fun for some strange reason. But living with my widow and her five kids wasn't fun. We'd only been married eight or nine months when I told her, 'Look, I'm sorry but I made a mistake. I'm not cut out to be a stepfather. I'm not in love with you. I want out.'

"She wasn't exactly wild about the idea of giving me a divorce, especially since I'd dragged her and her five kids from their familiar surroundings into the backwoods of northern Michigan. But she had little choice, so she agreed to a divorce.

"By this time I was in the last stages of alcoholism, climbing on the wagon for a month or so, then falling off harder than ever. In spite of my drinking problem, however, I was trying to get my license as a real estate salesman.

"One night I went to a tavern in the little town of Gas City, Indiana, and it was a gasser all right.

"I met a go-go dancer there and I think it was the brevity of her costume that turned me on. Anyway, the sparks flew between us and we ended up having an affair. I discovered that though she was only twenty-four she'd already been married twice and had a young son.

"Through miscalculation she got pregnant, I offered to pay for an abortion and she refused to have one, so I did the honorable thing and married her. The wedding took place when she was eight months pregnant. I certainly wasn't in love with her by any stretch of the imagination.

"I remained married to that woman five years and once a year, at least, we had prolonged separations. I was beginning to come to grips with my own problems, which were legion, and I had no time to help her with her problems.

"One of my problems was acute obesity but the worst was alcoholism, though it was really a symptom of my deeper problem—selfishness, materialism, living only for myself and my own gratification.

"I joined Alcoholics Anonymous against my will. Actually, I was ordered to join, sentenced to join it, by the judge who tried me on a drunken driving charge. When I showed up at the next meeting of the local AA I discovered that the judge himself was a member!

"In my struggle with booze I learned a great deal about myself. There are four factors that every alcoholic must have in his or her thinking pattern, and I was a classic case.

"First of all, alcoholics must be very deceptive. They *must* be. How are you going to hide the booze you have unless you're a liar? I was a pathological liar.

"Secondly, I haven't met a single alcoholic who wasn't sensitive—ranging from very sensitive to hypersensitive—to any form of criticism. They have no self-criticism and they can't accept it from anybody else, even when it's manifestly justified.

"Alcoholics also have extremely active, and often overly active, materialistic imaginations. If a clergyman is an alcoholic—and he's supposed to have a deeper appreciation than other people of spiritual values—you'll find that he's the type of cleric who is really working hard at building up a large congregation, and the home that goes with it, and the car, and the whole bit. He is materialistically minded.

"The fourth factor that you invariably find in the alcoholic is a deep, surging, burning resentment. Life has given him a raw deal. And maybe in some cases, it *has*. Maybe there's justification for the feeling of resentment.

But justified or not, it's there. And intuitively, these people who resent other people and life in general will produce situations where the resentment can be expressed.
They delight in displaying their anger, discontent and
bitterness.

"I had these four factors in spades. And before I licked
my alcoholism I had to come to understand the demons
that were driving me. Then there had to be a spiritual
change.

"One invaluable tool in helping me understand myself
was the study of graphoanalysis. I took up the study originally because I thought I could make money out it—
eventually I became a certified graphoanalyst, of which
I'm proud—but by the honest scrutiny of my own hand-
writing, as I went through the course, I discovered what a
rotten human being I was. A conceited, deceitful, hypersensitive phony.

"Believe me, I had so little previous insight into my own
character that these self-revelations hit me hard. They
were overwhelming. There were times when I cried myself to sleep because I'd discovered some new streak of
rottenness in me that previously I'd been blind to. It's incredible how revelatory graphoanalysis was to me.

"Anyway, to return to my marital history, my wife and
I mutually agreed to get a divorce and we did. She kept
our daughter. In recent years my ex-wife and I have become pretty good friends and I see my daughter often.

"Actually, my fifth wife was one of the best things that
ever happened to me. It was through that marriage, and
her occasional flings with other men, that I overcame my
abnormal jealousy. The growing insight I got from graphoanalysis helped me to understand, finally, that I didn't
own any woman, even if she was my wife.

"She was a person, just as I was, and she had the right
to be herself, whether or not it pleased me. When the divorce came, I felt no bitterness, just sorrow that I hadn't

been able to take time away from my own problems in order to help my wife cope with hers.

"My sixth marital venture occurred when I married a woman slightly older than myself who held a very responsible job and was very, very respectable. We met through our mutual interest in graphoanalysis, and by this time I was learning something about ESP, which also fascinated her.

"I had a deep attraction to this woman, mentally, physically and spiritually, and we married.

"That marriage dissolved after a year or so, mainly I think because it became quite evident to me that my wife was determined to remake me—not that I can blame her for wanting to try—into a more acceptable image. She taught me, or tried to, the social graces which I strikingly lacked. And she also became fascinated with the idea of catapulting me to fame and fortune as a psychic, whether I wanted that or not. You see, by this time quite a lot had happened inside of me. I'll explain later just what had happened but suffice it to say here that I was into self-hypnosis and largely through it conquered my alcoholism, reduced my weight to normal so that I no longer felt like a human blimp, and my ESP was also blossoming.

"But I didn't want to be pushed into anything I wasn't ready for. So my wife and I divorced. I just walked out of the marriage.

"I had developed my trance state by this time and I think one remark my wife made was very revealing of her attitude and possibly what was wrong with the marriage. She said: 'You know, you're so much nicer in trance than you are awake.'

"My seventh—and I sincerely believe it will be my last —marital venture started when I needed a conductor, someone to put me in and take me out of trance. The readings had stressed that the role of the conductor in these psychic sessions was just as important as mine! The wrong person, with the wrong vibes, if you like, made me emotionally and physically ill after a reading.

"At any rate, I met a young lady, twenty-five years my junior, in Bloomington, Indiana. I had by this time developed my psychic sensitivity to the point where I could sense an honest person, a loving person, or a phony. This young lady struck me as being very special. In fact, she seemed too good to be true.

"She was a student at the University of Indiana and an excellent student, as she always had been. She came from a very affluent Jewish home.

"When we met, she was a spiritual seeker. She had rejected materialistic values and was living in the country cooking on a wood stove and doing manual labor that she'd never done in her life. She was a very spiritually minded young woman.

"Frankly, I thought she would turn me down when I asked her to be my conductor and traveling companion (because by now I was holding psychic sessions in many different places). To my astonishment and delight Irva agreed to join me. She said she believed the readings were of immense importance to mankind and she wanted to help spread the message.

"It was six months before I got up the nerve to ask her to marry me. I had a rotten track record as a husband, which I had told her all about. There was the difference in our ages, in our social backgrounds.

"I was afraid she would say no but also afraid she would say yes. If she said no, I felt that she'd be frightened away and I would lose the companionship which had come to mean so much to me, because I did love her deeply. But if she said yes, I was tormented by the possibility that I might hurt her as I'd hurt my other wives and make a mess of this marriage too. And the thought of that was unbearable to me.

"Oddly enough, however, I had met the famous psychic

Peter Hurkos about six years ago in Chicago and he got a flash about me and said, 'Your first wife was Jewish and your last one will be also.' Well, my first legal wife—legal in American eyes—was the Jewish girl from Detroit. And now here was Irva, another Jewish girl whom I wanted desperately to marry.

"Maybe Hurkos' prophecy gave me the courage to ask Irva but anyway I did. And Irva said yes. The difference in our ages meant nothing to her, she said, and she had come to believe even more deeply in the spiritual importance of my psychic work. And, she added, she loved me.

"So we were married and we intend it to be forever. We now have a baby girl, Zoë, and I am honestly able to say that I have never known such peace, such joy, such fulfillment as I've found with my beloved Irva."

This brief recital of Ross Peterson's personal history explains, I think, the chapter title, "The *Unlikely* Seer." Sexual promiscuity. Alcoholism. Multiple divorces. Assault and battery. These hardly seem the stuff of which Edgar Cayces are made.

But what is as revealing, and even more important, than the outward events you've just read about is the *spiritual* odyssey of Ross Peterson—the things that were going on inside him all this time. The things that turned a human rimless zero into a wise, compassionate, loving man and a great psychic.

Now comes that part of the story . . .

Chapter Three

THE MAKING OF A SEER

The osteopath who introduced Ross Peterson to hypnosis also suggested yoga.

That ancient Eastern discipline of mind and body, he said, would help strengthen the back which had been "irreparably" injured in the fall from the truck.

In yoga, Peterson discovered another tool to change his body and his mind.

At this point, let him take up the story of his dramatic spiritual and psychic metamorphosis.

"The actual yoga exercises improved my back to the point where it no longer bothers me at all, though I was told that, medically speaking, I would never again have a normal spine. Recent X-rays have shown that my spine is now virtually normal.

"It was also through yoga that I began shedding some of the 263 pounds, by actual measure, of flab that I was then lugging around. In short order, I lost twenty-five pounds.

"But what really peeled off the pounds, and enabled me to keep them off—my steady weight now is 187 pounds, normal for a man six foot one and big-boned—was my continuing use of self-hypnosis.

"This success further convinced me that through hypnosis I could change my whole life; the way I thought, felt and acted. That I could turn my going-nowhere life around and become a winner instead of a loser.

"Then the thought occurred to me: Could you earn your living as a hypnotist? The idea of using the magic of the mind to help people, and getting paid for it, excited me.

"I checked and found that there were no state laws in Michigan regulating the use of hypnosis. I didn't need a college degree to become a professional hypnotist, just the training.

"I attended the Minneapolis School of Hypnosis and later took advanced courses in Chicago with the Association for the Advancement of Ethical Hypnosis, of which I became a member.

"Then I opened a small clinic in Lansing which I called the Lansing Hypnosis Center. It was a modest operation—two rooms and a receptionist and myself—but from the first I had some remarkable successes with clients.

"However, I wasn't exactly swamped with clients, which gave me plenty of time to pursue my training in self-hypnosis.

"Certain experiences had convinced me that the deeper I went into hypnosis, the more psychic I would become. If I could achieve the auto-hypnotic deep trance level, I suspected that my psychic powers would be immensely heightened.

"Actually, while I was putting my clients under hypnosis I often put myself under too and received, as well as gave, the positive suggestions I was using in the treatment.

"You see, what most people don't understand is that a person who is accomplished in self-hypnosis can go into the hypnotic state and continue to converse and act in a perfectly normal fashion, though his unconscious is wide open to suggestion.

"So what I would do was put my client into a very deep state of hypnosis, then let myself drop down to the hypnotic level too. And while I was giving positive suggestions to the client, I was also *receiving* them.

"It was while doing this that one day I had a spectacular psychic perception. I had put into a deep trance a young woman with an obesity problem who at the beginning of the therapy sessions had complained about lack of money to pay my fee and then suddenly stopped complaining and money no longer seemed a problem.

"Suddenly my mind was filled with a picture of her with her hand in a cash register, in the till. The feeling, which I can't describe, hit me so strongly inside that I *knew* this was true. I just knew.

"After the session, when she paid me, I couldn't help blurting out, 'You know, if your boss finds you stealing, you won't be back for any more hypnosis.'

"She turned red, began to stammer and then poured out the story. She had gotten a job as a cashier in a store in a shopping mall and was regularly filching money from the cash register.

"After she left it struck me: How did I know that? It was a lot stronger than a hunch.

"A couple of days later I had a woman client who complained of anxiety attacks stemming from her husband's sexual infidelities. And the anxiety made her overeat and she was fat.

"Well, about the second session I had her in deep hypnosis and then dropped myself into my usual light trance —that was all I was capable of at the time, a light hypnotic state—and suddenly I got another psychic flash. Again it hit me so hard I knew it was true. It was more than a mere hunch.

"What I saw, or felt, was that it wasn't this woman's husband who was unfaithful to her but she who was unfaithful to him! In fact, incredible as it seemed, I felt very strongly that she had had sexual relations with no less than eleven men that very week!

"Was that possible? It seemed wildly unlikely. Yet the feeling was so strong that I said, 'Why are you lying to me about your husband? The cause of your anxieties is your own sexual infidelity, which amounts to nymphomania.'

"Well, she broke down and confessed it was true, even to the eleven men from a nearby military barracks that she had bedded down with in the previous week.

"I told her her problem was too deep-seated for me to handle and urged her to see a psychiatrist. But again, how did I know? This time I knew it went far beyond a hunch.

"On another occasion a woman came to see me from a little town in Michigan and she was rather apprehensive about this hypnosis mumbo jumbo, though she obviously hoped it would help her insomnia. She asked if she could bring a witness. I said of course.

"She brought her teen-aged daughter and, as it turned out, the daughter was a much better hypnotic subject than her mother. While the woman went into only a medium state of hypnosis, the girl, sitting listening to the suggestions, spontaneously dropped into a profound somnambulistic trance. So we decided that at the next visit the daughter would wait in the reception room.

"However, during the second session, when I had the mother in medium hypnosis, I opened the door to give my receptionist a message I'd forgotten earlier and there was the daughter, slumped in her chair in a deep sleep. A somnambulistic trance.

"I told the mother about this and at the next visit proposed an experiment.

"'Let me not put you under hypnosis at all,' I suggested, 'but you just sit here wide awake while I *think* hypnotic suggestions at your daughter.'

"Now, the girl, remember, was sitting outside the office, which was soundproof, and couldn't have overheard our conversation. But when I opened the door a few minutes later, there she was. Sound asleep, in a somnambulistic trance.

"It was then I realized, or strongly suspected, that I was hypnotizing the girl telepathically, by merely thinking the suggestions into her mind. This was a shattering discovery for me. The mind could communicate directly with another mind, without words being spoken.

"I also noted a correlation between my hypnotic depth, which varied from one to four, say, on a scale of ten, and the clarity and accuracy of my psychic flashes. The deeper I was, the clearer and more detailed the flashes. This is what made me strive for the auto-hypnotic trance. If I reached that state I hoped, my psychic powers might explode!

"Anyway, my flashes, which came with increasing frequency, and my growing understanding that the mind could penetrate physical barriers and cross space—as when I telepathically hypnotized the girl in another room—all these things were prompting some radical changes in my thinking.

"From never having thought about man having a soul, I

now found myself more than half convinced that man *was* a soul and had a body. The mind, I was coming to see, was infinitely greater than the body.

"Then came an experience that introduced me to another facet of the psychic world which was destined to become very important to me: reincarnation.

"I knew virtually nothing about the subject at this point but I was propelled into it when I tried to help a patient overcome his problem of lifelong stuttering. I achieved very little success with him. Finally, I decided to try an age regression—to take the young man back in his mind to the traumatic experience which had caused his stuttering. If we found that, we could probably solve the root problem.

"Because of my relative inexperience, I lost control of the regression and the subject went back past childhood to infancy, to birth, and then he just kept on going until he said he was floating around in space with a different kind of body from his physical one.

"I was frightened and got him back to present time as fast as I could. That was the end of any further age regressions for me for quite a while.

"But the experience had piqued my curiosity. Did memories extend back not only to the womb but beyond? And if so, beyond to *what*? A life before conception?

"This was another mind-blowing thought for me. Life before birth. Life in another body, different from the physical. What sort of body could that be? Or had the subject just fantasized it all?

"I began reading the literature voraciously and found that there was plenty of evidence that memory goes back to the womb, before birth. And there were some reputable investigators, I discovered, who believed that unconscious memory went back to previous lives. In other words, reincarnation—living more than one life on this earth—was true.

"I got to know some people from the Michigan ESP Research Association who brought me up to date about what was happening in parapsychology. I told them about my psychic flashes and they put me through some ESP card-guessing tests, such as J. B. Rhine used at Duke University.

"I took the tests cold, not under hypnosis but in a normal state of consciousness. They indicated that I was what ESP researchers call a 'goat.' Those who score high on the ESP card-guessing tests are 'sheep.' The people who tested me said that I should forget about trying to be psychic because I just didn't have it. I was a goat if ever there was one.

"Why I didn't repeat the tests in the hypnotic state, I don't really know. Possibly because I found the card guessing a little silly and removed from life. I didn't want to guess cards. I wanted to read minds, to travel through time and space, to scan past, present and future. I thought the ESP cards were Mickey Mouse stuff.

"Anyway, at this point a friend gave me a copy of a book entitled *There Is a River* by Thomas Sugrue. It was about Edgar Cayce.

"Now I had become a voracious reader, because I realized how ignorant I was, and I was plowing through everything I could find about the mind—books on suggestion, hypnosis, ESP and so on. In fact, I was devouring about a book every other day.

"But that book by Sugrue hit me hard. Because I have some of the man from Missouri in me, as most people have, and when I read about the meticulous documentation of Cayce's powers I was impressed. I found myself believing not only in his medical readings but in all the rest of what he taught while in trance—reincarnation, the law of karma or perfect justice, the evolution of the soul, and his whole spiritual philosophy. It made sense to me.

And his verified medical readings seemed to me to credential his past-life readings.

"In other words, if Cayce was right when he diagnosed some person unknown to him as having leukemia, why shouldn't he be right when he attributed the illness to the man's having been a bloodthirsty executioner in a previous life? He had gleefully shed other men's blood. Now he had come back to symbolically shed his own blood. That made sense to me. It made sense of why some people suffered more than others. The whole idea of karma—that we reap in one life what we sowed in a previous one—rang a bell with me. I found it eminently reasonable.

"But the thing about the Cayce book that struck me more than anything else, and stuck in my mind, was Cayce's own statement, time and time again, that *anybody* could learn to do what he did, if only they applied themselves. I couldn't get this out of my mind.

"I resolved, God being my helper, that I was going to become someone who could do what Cayce did. I had three motives.

"The first was an honest one: I wanted to be a better counselor, to help people in a way that went far beyond what I was already doing. This was an utterly sincere passion with me.

"The second reason was less lofty. I had a need to be always right and I felt that becoming like Cayce would make me infallible. This was an ego bit that I had to get over. It was painful but I finally did conquer it and not until then did things really begin to happen.

"My third motive was materialistic: I could charge larger fees because I was going to be able to give people so much more than hypnosis. And with more money, I could live better.

"So I read several more books on Mr. Cayce. I joined a psychical research group in Lansing. I began to learn what meditation was all about. I read books on astral

travel out of the body. And after I had read eighty or
ninety books on a variety of psychic subjects I discovered
they were all saying the same thing: You had to practice,
to work like hell, or heaven, to achieve the altered state of
consciousness in which these wonderful things happened.

"So then I started in earnest perfecting my auto-hyp-
nosis. I strove desperately to achieve a very, very deep
somnambulistic trance in which the ego, the conscious
mind, gave up and the unconscious took over.

"It took me two years of unremitting effort, and a lot of
painful self-purging, before I hit the jackpot.

"The first thing I did was to devote an hour a day to
self-hypnosis. I would lay back in my Lazy Boy chair. I
began by relaxing the body, as I had learned to do in
yoga. I soon reached the point where I understood that
the body can be fully relaxed and tension-free and yet the
mind is fully active.

"I started my relaxation from the head down, beginning with the scalp, the forehead, the eyes, the cheeks,
the jaws, the ears . . . I divided the body into as many
segments as I could and spent time relaxing each segment
before moving on to the next one.

"I gave the suggestions mentally to myself. And eventually I reached a stage where, though I knew I had a
body, I honestly couldn't have said, if I'd been asked,
where my finger, knee or abdomen was.

"To get to that stage took about seven months of daily
practice.

"The next seven or eight months were spent in relaxing
the mind—I had gotten the body relaxed but the mind
was still very active—and this part was much, much
harder. Quieting the mind, annihilating the ego, was
much more difficult than quieting the body.

"But I persisted with blood, toil, sweat and tears. Every
time a stray thought came into my mind, I cleared it out,
erased it, as though I were brushing chalk off a black-

board. I tried to concentrate on what we normally see when we first shut our eyes—a void. I concentrated on that void and sought to enter into it, to be swallowed up by it. No thoughts. No pictures. Just the void.

"I believe I began to achieve a deep hypnoidal state when after a minute or two of just seeing blackness, the void, without any vagrant thoughts or images intruding, suddenly my inner vision would be filled with a kaleidoscope of color. But primarily a deep blue edged in gold in an ovoid shape. Almost like an embryo.

"It didn't move or shimmer. It was just there, a blue ovoid ringed with gold.

"The next step was when I realized that I was losing my sense of time. I would focus on this golden bluish embryo and not know how much time had elapsed.

"I began to become aware that I was staring at this blue ovoid edged in gold and then the next thing I knew I was waking up, with no sense of time having passed. Sometimes I'd find I had been out for a half-hour; other times, five minutes. But it all seemed the same. I had achieved a state of timelessness.

"On several occasions I spent as long as two hours in this timeless state and couldn't believe it when I awakened and realized just how long I'd been under.

"Then I started using thirty-minute tape cassettes of my own voice to ask myself questions while I was under and to give me the suggestion to awaken.

"At first I asked selfish questions of myself, like about my physical health. Then I asked for prognostications about what was going to happen to me in my job, my marriage and so on.

"Later, I would play back the cassettes and be amazed to hear this voice, which was me but didn't sound like me, giving answers to the questions I asked. It was a kind of eerie experience. Me talking to myself, telling myself things I didn't know on the conscious level.

"My language in the deep trance state wasn't like my normal speech. It was flowery, rhetorical—King James English—much the way Cayce had spoken when he was in trance. Maybe this is the native language of the unconscious. Anyway, it didn't sound like me when I was awake.

"The answers I got weren't too damn sensible in the beginning because of their brevity. Or abruptness would be a better word. I discovered that you got back only what you asked for.

"Once I asked, 'Is vanity my big problem?' and the trance answer was 'yes.' Hell, I knew that. What I wanted to know was what to do about it. Then I realized that I had to ask for *that* if that was what I wanted: How can I overcome my vanity?

"You see, the unconscious is like a computer in this respect. You get back from it only what you put in. If you ask a question that can be answered yes or no, you'll probably get a yes or no answer. The more complex the question, the richer and fuller the answer.

"Then I had two close friends who began doing for me what Cayce's wife had done for him: they acted as my conductors. They used suggestions to put me under, asked the questions while I was under, and then brought me out. They worked with me for several months and we started getting rather startling results.

"The readings said that the conductor was crucial to the success of the session. A mean, spiteful person acting as conductor, the readings warned, could make me physically ill when I came out of trance. And I had occasions when that happened. So it is very important to have a kind, attentive, empathetic and loving person as conductor.

"The readings told me to pray before entering the trance. The prayer, which I use faithfully, was, 'Dear

Lord, please help me to help these people. Not my will but Thine be done.'

"Then we were told that the conductor should use a prayer and a set formula for taking me under. This never varies. It goes: 'Dear Lord, please protect this entity from all negative influences, regardless of source, and give us the answers we seek of this inquiring mind through the manifestation of truth, intelligence and love. Amen. Would you please allow your mind to go to whom, to where, to what, and to when it is directed.'

"Then I might be directed to go backward in time ten thousand years to Atlantis—which I've done, and we have a wealth of material on that—or forward in time to predict the outcome of a business deal. Or I might, as is usually the case, simply be told to locate the form of so-and-so at such-and-such an address—I seem to need the address to get a fix on the person—and report on the health of the entity. Most of the readings are health readings but many touch on past lives too, because present illnesses and other conditions are often rooted in past causes. I mean causes generated in previous earth lives.

"You know, I haven't told this to anybody, but just before I plunge into the void of total unconsciousness, I see eight faces in a semicircle coming toward me.

"There are five men and three women. They look like everyday people. Except for another one, the ninth one, who is about five times as large as the others and looms up behind them. He's a patriarchal figure, old with a white beard and a flowing robe.

"I feel love radiating from these nine, but sometimes disapproval too if I've misbehaved or haven't wanted to go into trance. Sometimes, you know, the readings give me hell for not living up to all the light I've received. But even the reproof has the feel of love about it.

"I've never asked for the names of these people—never

felt it was necessary—but I feel that they're my guides, my angels.

"What the readings have said is that they are those with whom I made a pact, before I entered the physical body in this incarnation, to seek help when I needed it. Their part of the pact is to provide help when called on.

"It took a long time for me to ask. But that was my fault."

Chapter Four

THE SEER MEETS A PSYCHOLOGIST

It appears that Dr. Lee Pulos was known to Ross Peterson, psychically, before the two ever met.

That, at least, is one interpretation of a psychic reading which Peterson gave in Toronto on May 22, 1974.

In that reading, which was for another individual, the entranced seer predicted that the person in question would be helped by "one of a Greek-sounding name. He will be that of the gourmet in the preparation of foods. And he will offer this one the opportunity to move the body in the geographical westerly direction . . . Whether this one takes the opportunity is his choice but it will be an opportunity to build that which is part of his destiny . . ."

As it happened, within a few days Lee Pulos ("one of a Greek-sounding name"), who besides being a professor of behavioral sciences is also a restaurateur running an international chain of fabulously successful Spaghetti Factories ("He will be that of the gourmet in the preparation of foods"), out of the blue walked into the office in Toronto where Peterson had given the reading.

The upshot was that a business partnership was formed between Pulos and the individual for whom the reading had been given. And the partnership involved that individual's moving from Toronto to Vancouver, on Canada's west coast ("he will offer this one the opportunity to move the body in the geographical westerly direction").

When Lee Pulos first met Peterson, the latter gave him a penetrating glance and said coolly: "You and I will be working together within twelve months."

"At the time," recalls Pulos, "I said to myself, 'Who the hell is this guy anyway? What does he think he is, psychic?'

"Well," the psychologist added with a wry chuckle, "in eight months Ross and I were working very closely together. In fact, he lived for a while in my home."

Lee Pulos is a trained scientist (Ph.D. in clinical psychology from the University of Denver) who serves as assistant clinical professor in the department of psychiatry at the University of British Columbia. His specialties are hypnotherapy and group therapy, in both of which he has a private practice.

Pulos has had several psychic readings with Ross Peterson and has studied the results of his work closely. How does he rate his accuracy?

"I would say that when Ross does physical readings, health readings, he is in the 90 to 95 per cent accuracy range. I speak here from personal experience," the psychologist said in an interview.

"Let me tell you what happened. It's so incredible I can still hardly believe it myself.

"The first reading took place in 1974. Ross, at the time, knew nothing about me. We had just met.

"He went into his trance—I call it his 'stoned' state—and he immediately picked up the fact that I had a bad knee, for which I used to have to wear a brace following knee surgery. He also zeroed in on an enlarged prostate, which was absolutely true, as I knew from a recent medical examination.

"He said that I had a mild curvature of the spine, which was true. I was suffering low back pain. Moreover, he prescribed yoga exercises to correct that problem. The directions were quite specific. I was told to do one exercise that involved bringing my feet back and touching my toes behind my head . . . very, very slowly bringing my feet back and touching them behind my head. Sounds crazy, but it worked.

"The other exercise has me sit in a kind of half-lotus position, with my arms up, and rotate my torso slowly one way, gradually increasing the degree of rotation, and then do the same in the opposite direction.

"I followed these exercises, and still do, and my back pains are virtually a thing of the past. And I play raquetball better than ever!

"But the really spectacular detail of Ross's reading was when he said, 'This body has had an early injury to the gonads.'

"Well, so far as I was concerned this was totally wrong. But I said to Ross, 'You're batting four out of five, which ain't bad.' I was truly impressed by the overall accuracy of the reading, but the remark about an injured gonad I counted as an absolute error.

"Until almost a year later. Then, I had a pain in my

right testicle. I went to the doctor. He said, 'How old are you? We operate tomorrow,' which scared the hell out of me. I thought it was 'hello, good-by,' for sure.

"Anyway, the next thing I remember was the doctor coming to me after I came out of the anesthetic and he was smiling.

"'You're O.K.,' he said. 'Don't worry, it wasn't cancer. It was a hydrocele.'

"When I got my senses about me, I said, 'What the hell is a hydrocele?'

"The urologist said, 'Well, when you were an embryo, *in utero,* the gonads descended, as they do in normal development, but in your case, in the process of descending, a micro-mini air pocket formed and that was the beginning of the hydrocele.' And forty-seven years later, I ended up on the surgeon's table having it corrected.

"As I now am aware, a hydrocele is a cavity in the body that fills with serous fluid. Basically it's a fluid pocket that causes pain and often swelling, and it must be drained of fluid for the problem to be cured.

"When I told my urologist that a year before, a psychic, Ross Peterson, had told me of an early injury to the gonads, and intimated that it was going to cause me trouble—well, that urologist just flipped! There's no way that could have been inference, guesswork, deduction or anything but pure clairvoyance, because nobody—not even me—knew that the injury had occurred. And forty-seven years before.

"But that isn't the end of Ross's amazing performances with me. On December 23, 1975, I developed another chronic soreness in my right testicle, the same one that had had the hydrocele. And I thought, 'Oh no! Maybe my luck has run out this time.' Because remember, it had been almost a year since the surgery.

"So I called Ross in Michigan—I was traveling and was in Ottawa at the time—and I said, 'Look, I'm really concerned. It's a soreness in the same testicle and I would really like you to check it out. I'm seeing the doctor as soon as I get back home to Vancouver but see what you come up with in the meantime.'

"So Ross, in that cool way of his, asked me my exact location and I gave him the address where I would be in Ottawa at a certain precise time. He said he would do the reading and to call back for the results.

"Well, I called later and the first thing his wife Irva told me was that the reading started out by giving me hell for not drinking a little wine with my meals.

" 'We have told this body to drink a small portion of wine before each meal because he needs it to help him relax and aid digestion.'

"Imagine! Here was something I'd been told almost a year before and it comes out again. And it was correct, I hadn't been drinking the wine.

"And it said, sort of, oh, by the way, that I had nothing to worry about. The soreness in the testicle was related to the surgery and Ross used a rather technical term for it which I forget. He also prescribed a certain treatment (which I didn't follow) using camphor oil and castor oil packs. However, he said the condition would clear up completely on its own.

"When I got back to Vancouver and went to my favorite urologist, he checked me out and used almost exactly the same terminology Ross had and said the soreness was merely transitory and was connected with the previous surgery.

"So Ross had scored another bull's-eye!"

Lee Pulos is not the only member of his family to have had a shattering experience with Ross Peterson. His brother's first reading with Peterson was, if possible, even more extraordinary than Lee's.

"My brother, Andy, went initially to Ross out of curios-

ity. He was skeptical. He had past-life readings done for
himself and his son, which were very interesting. They
seemed to fit many of the idiosyncrasies of character and
personality of both my brother and his son, and explained
these in terms of karmic carry-overs from previous lifetimes. They had a ring of truth.

"Anyway, my brother also asked Ross to do a health
reading on both his wife and his daughter Nadine, who
was ten.

"Ross said there was something wrong in terms of his
wife's, Carol's, uterus. There was a diseased condition,
though not serious.

"Well, my brother Andy said, 'No, I'm sorry but I don't
think that's right.'

"Then Ross said that Nadine, the daughter, had a very
painful tooth which was actually abscessed and that the
poison was spreading through her jaw and the tooth must
be removed.

"And again, Andy demurred, 'Well, I don't think that's
right.'

"But Andy called Carol, his wife, the next day. (He
was in Toronto on business, I think, and she was at home
in Vancouver.)

"He said, 'How's everything?' And she replied, 'Oh, I
should have told you this, but I went to the doctor yesterday and he found a polyp in my uterus which he wants to
remove. Nothing serious.'

"'And how's Nadine?' Andy asked.

"'Well,' said Carol, 'yesterday we had to take her out
of school because she was screaming with pain. Turned
out she had an abscessed tooth and we rushed her to the
dentist and he removed it.'

"At this, my brother was almost in shock! How could
Ross Peterson, in trance, some three thousand miles away,
have picked up correctly both the physical conditions of
his wife and his daughter? And so specifically! An

abscessed tooth is more than your run-of-the-mill coincidence."

As a businessman, as well as a behavioral scientist, Lee Pulos has used Ross Peterson's psychic gifts for practical advice. And, he says, it has proven enormously helpful.

"We asked Ross, in a reading, what the prospects were for a new eating place we were planning to open in Toronto called the Organ Grinder. It was different from anything we'd done and we had our doubts about whether it would succeed.

"The reading said the Organ Grinder would be *very* successful and to proceed with no doubts whatsoever.

"Well, in four months it turned into the second most successful operation in our whole international chain of restaurants. In just four months! That's pretty phenomenal.

"We also used Ross in personnel selection. We had a reading and told Ross in trance that we were considering several people for managership of restaurants and asked him to assess their suitability. Then I gave him the names and their addresses and he started to tell us about them.

"He's been incredibly accurate. In one reading he said that a young man we were considering for managership, but had real doubts about, was very honest but needed close supervision. The problem, said Ross, 'is that this one does not know figures. Not in the least. He cannot add two and two.'

"We found that this was absolutely true. The guy couldn't add two and two to save his life.

"Ross also said he had difficulty working with women because of his 'chauvinistic attitudes.' Well, he's from another country and he *is* very chauvinistic, though he's working on it.

"There's no way this sort of thing could be guesswork. It's too uncannily accurate too often.

"Once, I gave Ross the names of two employees with whom there were some problems and we asked him to clarify the situation. The pair were thousands of miles away, in a city Ross had never visited, but he started in describing the appearance of the restaurant, the trees in front of it, everything about it. He even described the appearance of one of the men whom, needless to say, he had never seen."

Lee Pulos intimated that the business readings are not as straightforward as the physical or health readings. There is a certain delphic ambiguity at times, he said, and nuances that can be misinterpreted.

"I know of one company which suspected that some hanky-panky was going on in one of its stores because the percentages were way out of whack. Ross did a reading and pointed his finger at two people in the store.

"The company confronted the pair and there was a hell of a furor and Ross's implications appeared to be inaccurate.

"However, later, one of the principals involved himself said, 'You know, Peterson may have been right after all,' and he proceeded to point out an individual in the store who could have been involved in something culpable but not in the way that Ross indicated. In other words, yes, there could have been things going out the back door but not in a dishonest way. There was incompetence rather than collusion. Ross actually had used a metaphor and it had to be read the right way to come up with the right answer.

"So, in certain areas, the readings speak metaphorically, cryptically, almost surrealistically. And if you take them literally and concretely, you'll misinterpret them."

Another problem in assessing the accuracy of Peterson's business or economic readings is that so much of them pertains to events still in the future.

"For example," said Lee Pulos, "Ross has given us

prognostications about long-term business trends, a wheat rust that's supposed to affect spaghetti production and a coming shortage of tomatoes. These all lie in the future. We'll have to wait and see what happens.

"I know of one prediction in which he was 100 per cent wrong. Absolutely, totally wrong."

Mistaken predictions, however, are to be expected from the very nature of time and futurity, as the readings describe them. The readings say repeatedly that only rarely, if ever, can the future be absolutely foretold.

"Even God does not know what thou might think to-morrow," the entranced Peterson once said.

Some events, a few, do seem to be fixed, fated if you like. But in large part the future, as described in the readings, is fluid, plastic, capable of taking many different forms depending on how people think and act in the present.

Skeptics might call it hedging when, in trance, Peterson says: "Considering the law of probabilities we can only say that in this case it appears very likely that . . ." But is it hedging, or simply a recognition that the future is largely contingent on the present?

Once, asked in a reading if "things will go well for this entity," Peterson replied: "Thou shouldst know that there is no man who can say that this or that *must* be so. For destiny is not lived until it *is* lived. And it is determined by the thoughts that thou holdest in thy mind today. For that which thou holdest in thy mind today, thy *prayer*—for that is what it really is—is that which will determine how thou rewardest or punisheth thyself on the morrow and the morrows. See?"

The health readings presuppose that free will can often change what otherwise would come to pass.

Often the readings have said: "This body will develop a serious imbalance unless certain dietary changes are made. If these are followed, illness can be avoided."

That's changing the future.

Or: "This entity will drive her spouse to divorce her unless she curbs her cutting tongue which continually complains. But if she changes her thinking, strives to be more loving, the spouse will respond and harmony can flourish once again between them."

Such admonitions suggest that, as the readings see it, the future is far from being fixed. It is at least partly in dynamic flux and decisions made in the here and now can change what otherwise would be.

As a psychologist and clinical hypnotist, Lee Pulos suggested how Ross Peterson does what he does.

"Basically it's a hypnotic function in which the rational, logical, analytical mind is turned off, as well as any interfering physical stimuli," Pulos said.

"Now, Ross told me that when he started doing it, on a scale of one to ten he was a three as a subject in terms of hypnotic depth. And he just kept at it and kept at it and suddenly, one day, he fell over the deep end and that was it.

"This is consistent with my experience in hypnosis— that hypnotic depth is not a fixed state. You can increase it. This is what Ross did. He just kept at it until he finally achieved it. And I feel that this is possible for anyone.

"I also feel that what goes on is that there is a subconscious-to-subconscious communication when he is in that state. Or possibly that he connects with some type of universal source, a collective unconscious, from which he selectively extracts information.

"Some psychics in trance claim to be taken over by spirit guides or patron saints, but I think this is an idiosyncratic or cultural phenomenon. I think the trance psychic is connecting with his own unconscious and through it, the unconscious minds of others, and possibly this universal pool of consciousness."

Asked if he would compare Ross Peterson to Edgar Cayce, Dr. Pulos said: "The phenomenon is essentially the same. I would say that Ross is 80 or 85 per cent as good as Cayce was. Cayce was superior, I think, in his general predictive powers. But who knows how far Ross will develop?"

Indeed. Who does?

Chapter Five

A MEDICAL ASSESSMENT OF THE SEER

Who would be the ideal arbiter to evaluate Ross Peterson's seership?

Since the slumbering seer, like his mentor, Edgar Cayce, majors in *medical* readings, a well-trained physician presumably would be needed to assess their accuracy. However, some, if not all, the readings also contain psychological insights and to evaluate these requires, ideally, an expert in the behavioral sciences.

A man who combines high qualifications both as a medical *and* a behavioral scientist has subjected Ross Peterson to intensive study. His name: Dr. F. Logan Stanfield.

He has checked out more than two score of the Peterson medical readings. And his findings?

"As a medical diagnostician," said Dr. Stanfield, "Ross Peterson is extremely accurate. He is, in fact, rarely wrong. In a word, he's phenomenal!"

What are the qualifications and background of this scientist who has had a unique opportunity to study in depth a contemporary version of Edgar Cayce?

Logan Stanfield began his career as a mechanical engineer, earning a bachelor's and master's degree in that field from Newark College of Engineering and New York University respectively. He received his medical degree from Howard University in 1952 and then took the equivalent of six years of specialized training in psychiatry and psychoanalysis at New York Medical College, and Bellevue Medical Center's psychiatric division, graduating from the Comprehensive Course in Psychoanalysis. He is a certified psychoanalyst.

Besides maintaining a private practice in psychoanalysis, Dr. Stanfield has held a variety of professional posts. He served as an instructor in psychiatry at New York Medical College, was Assistant Chief of the Adult Out-Patient Psychiatric Clinic of New York's Mt. Sinai Hospital, and Psychiatrist-in-Charge of the Adolescent and Adult Narcotics Addiction Service at Metropolitan Hospital, New York. For three years he was consultant psychiatrist to the IBM Corporation in the New York City area.

Academically and professionally Logan Stanfield has the highest distinctions. He is a diplomate of the American Board of Psychiatry and Neurology, a Fellow of the Academy of Psychoanalysis, and a member or former member of thirteen professional societies. He is licensed to practice medicine in four states of the United States and two provinces of Canada. From 1954 to 1971 he had a private practice in psychiatry and psychoanalysis on New

York's Fifth Avenue. Since then he has been in private practice in Toronto, Ontario.

It was in Toronto that Logan Stanfield met Ross Peterson. For the archetypal man of science the meeting was a shattering introduction to the unfamiliar and eerie world which lies beyond the physical senses. Since that initial encounter Dr. Stanfield has studied and evaluated numerous Peterson readings to determine how they checked out.

"I've followed up at least fifty of the readings," the psychoanalyst said, "and the results are, to say the least, extremely impressive.

"In each case I ordered a specific diagnostic test focusing on the particular organ system in the body where Ross said there was a malfunction. For example, if he cited a hyperthyroid, or overactive thyroid condition, I immediately sent that person for thyroid function tests. If the reading mentioned a tendency toward diabetes I had the relevant procedures done—glucose tolerance test, blood sugar levels taken while eating and after fasting, and so on.

"In other words, I have had ample opportunity to examine many patients with the classical methods of medical science, zeroing in on the particular bodily area where the reading detected a malfunction. And I must say, from a medical point of view, that Ross Peterson is very, very accurate. Uncannily so.

"Without getting into a technical statistical breakdown at this time, I would estimate that he has been correct in his diagnoses nine times out of ten, or nineteen out of twenty, if you like. That is an exceedingly high level of accuracy, astronomically beyond chance.

"In a number of cases I've referred people to a chiropractor for spinal X-rays and these have revealed subluxations—variations in the distance between adjacent vertebrae—and rotations—angular displacements or tilting of

the vertebrae—matching precisely those pinpointed by
Ross in the readings. He is *minutely* accurate in describing these spinal misalignments, which the readings say
have a marked effect on the individual's health."

Besides assessing Peterson medically, Logan Stanfield
has had a chance to watch his performance in other, nonmedical areas.

"Yes," he went on, "I've been in a position, a unique
one, I think, to appraise his general prophetic abilities.
My appraisal has been on the basis of specific predictions
he made about individuals who either were in continuing
psychoanalysis with me or whom I otherwise was able to
follow up.

"In the area of forecasting events of a nonmedical nature I would say that Ross has been correct—oh, at the *absolute* minimum—six times out of ten. Mind you, I'm
speaking here of predictions of specific events or series of
events, not mere generalities. Some of his predictions
have been strikingly accurate, almost unbelievably so.

"Taking an overview, then, based on at least two years'
association with Ross Peterson, my considered judgment
is that he has demonstrated unequivocally psychic powers
of an astonishingly high order. Frankly, he's amazing. At
first, I admit that I was somewhat awestruck by the incredible things he does."

But Peterson is not infallible. ("Thank God!" expostu-
lated one sitter. "If he were, that would be too much. He
wouldn't be human. He'd be terrifying!") Dr. Stanfield
has documented cases in which the seer struck out completely.

"In at least two instances," said the psychoanalyst,
"Ross completely missed the patient's illness. In one case
he correctly diagnosed a tumor of the brain but called it a
'fibroid mass,' which is benign, whereas it already had
been medically diagnosed as a highly malignant tumor,
which ultimately proved to be lethal. In that case Ross

also missed the fact that the brain tumor had metasta-
sized, or spread from a primary lesion in the lung. Ross
insisted that the lung was clear, even in the face of my
statement that X-rays had revealed a growth there. He
was completely off."

Why the misses?

Dr. Stanfield has some theories about this problem, involving body metabolism and its interaction with the central nervous system. But let us leave this important question for consideration later in the chapter.

Now let us re-experience, through the eyes and ears of
a sophisticated explorer of the psyche, his first encounter
with a human being who claims to be psychic when he
talks in his sleep.

"Before sitting with Ross Peterson," said Dr. Stanfield,
"though I had an interest in parapsychology, I had no
clear concept of what the field embraced. And I had
never sought out a psychic for a sitting.

"I went to see Ross because of the remarkable accuracy
of a reading he gave for a friend of mine. This friend,
whose judgment I respected, told me that he had asked
Ross about his estranged wife, who was in Los Angeles,
and Ross proceeded to describe her with hair-raising accuracy. The woman he described was unquestionably this
man's wife. Yet Peterson had never seen her, nor even my
friend before, and she at the time was some three thousand miles away.

"My friend was also concerned about a custody suit involving his daughter. Ross made a number of predictions
about how matters would proceed, going into considerable detail and laying out a timetable of events. Shortly
after, he proved to be astonishingly accurate in one of the
short-term predictions. And as the scenario has unfolded,
his predictions have continued to come true more or less
on schedule.

"Anyway, not surprisingly, as a prober of the mind, I

felt my curiosity aroused and arranged for a sitting with this psychic, clairvoyant, seer or whatever he called himself.

"Entering his office, I met a white-haired man, dark in complexion, tall, with strange eyes that seemed to have silver flecks around the periphery of the irises. He was gentle, well-mannered and spoke in a quiet voice, though there was power in it.

"We chatted for a few minutes about inconsequential things, then I saw a woman setting up a tape recorder. She, I was told, was the conductor who would induct Ross into the trance. Since I wanted a private reading, the conductor agreed to leave the room after she had put Ross in trance; after she had turned on the radio, so to speak.

"Then Ross settled down in his lounge-type chair, which allowed him to recline in an almost horizontal position, and calmly prepared to go into trance. Having used hypnosis extensively in my practice, I watched very closely.

"Frankly, what happened was very moving. The room seemed charged with a steadily building energy. I had the strange feeling, as he progressed obviously into a deeper and deeper trance, that he was attracting forces or emanations from somewhere outside himself. There was something, well, unearthly about the whole thing.

"At that point the conductor said to Ross, 'Please clear the mind,' and he responded, in this utterly different voice, *The mind is clear.*'

"Then the conductor got up and departed, leaving me alone with this somnambulistic psychic.

"Candidly speaking, I was shaken by the difference between Peterson's normal voice and his trance voice. It was actually *eerie*. It gave one the impression that there *was* another presence than Peterson.

"Well, following prior instructions, I mentioned the

name and address of my son and asked Ross to locate him.

"All the while, I had been carefully observing the oscillation of Peterson's eyeballs beneath his closed lids—as though he were scanning a screen—and these eye movements now accelerated. Finally, out of his mouth came again that eerie voice. It said, *Yes, we have the form.*'

"He then proceeded to describe my son with striking accuracy, in terms of his temperament, his interests, experiences which he had just gone through and others which he would soon go through.

"He spoke of specific traits: my son's passion for sports; his desire to drive a racing car, which he's typically cut out for; and his love for flying. Well, I'm a pilot and my son does love to fly, so Ross was right on with every point.

"He also said that he detected in this boy, who was eight at the time, the inclination to become a healer, specifically a surgeon and still more specifically a neurosurgeon.

"He said that as a neurosurgeon my son would be utilizing instruments yet to be developed to remove lesions in the brain and central nervous system.

"He made the comment, 'This is what will be most meaningful to this entity for he has been a healer before,' implying a prior existence.

"Well, I have been very careful not to make this a self-fulfilling prophecy by steering my son, consciously or unconsciously, toward neurosurgery. But as I've watched him developing, Ross's prediction becomes more and more probable. In fact, I see nothing to contraindicate it.

"My son's mind is sharpening on a daily basis. He is interested in biology, in living systems. And he's very much interested in devices, electronics equipment, and so forth. Yes, I see a definite trend that could lead him very easily into neurosurgery.

"I also asked Ross about my daughter and he gave me a

similarly accurate description of her, stressing her maternal feelings, her desire to marry and have children, and her love of wide open spaces. There was no drive for a career in her, he said, and this was quite correct. Again, I could hear my daughter being profiled, and not somebody else. There were too many specific traits mentioned.

"Incidentally, and this is an interesting point, when I asked Ross to locate my daughter I gave the street address but neglected to add *Toronto, Ontario, Canada*. And in response, instead of giving me information, this human computer with the hollow voice asked, 'In what part of the world?'

"It was then the realization struck me that though I was sitting there, in Toronto, next to an inert form which appeared to be asleep, yet was capable of verbally responding to questions, Peterson's *mind* was somewhere else. His mind seemed to be wandering around in space pretty much as it pleased, capable of projecting itself to any designated spot on the globe. At least, that's what appeared to be happening.

"Anyway, I added the Toronto, Ontario, Canada, and Ross said, 'Ah yes, now we have the form,' and proceeded to describe her.

"Then came a bit of a shocker—something which shook me up more than what already had transpired.

"You see, for years I have been trying to understand the brain or the mind, however you express it, particularly its potential capabilities: what it really can and cannot do. For a long time I had suspected that such phenomena as hallucinations and delusions were not merely indicators of psychopathology but possibly clues to hidden capacities lurking beneath the surface of the mind.

"Now, in the reading with Ross Peterson, I was seeing some of my suspicions confirmed. Here before my eyes was evidence that mind is primary and the body secondary; that the mind has ways of perceiving which transcend the physical avenues of perception.

"That moment was a turning point in my life.

"And the real shocker, the moment of truth, as it were, was when I asked Ross to locate the form of my wife-to-be, giving the address. Now, she could have been doing anything on that particular afternoon, but instantly Peterson said, 'Yes, we have the form. *Sitting at a desk.*'

"That rocked me because I happened to know that at that very time she was sitting at a desk!

"So here was this unusual man, describing not only the location of a mind and body but even the anatomical position! It was as if he had X-ray eyes that could scan any distance and see through walls.

"In a number of readings since, I've heard Ross say things like, 'Yes, we have the form. What an odd time of day to be dressed in a bathrobe.' Or, 'The form is listening to the radio.' You get used to this after a while, but the first time it tends to stop you in your tracks.

"The reading included information about three prior incarnations of mine which Ross said were especially relevant to my present life.

"Now, I had always felt intuitively that human consciousness, the mind, survived biological death, and that reincarnation was a plausible form for such survival to take. But I hadn't dwelt on the subject and had no strong conviction, in any sense. There was merely a suspicion on my part that reincarnation was true.

"However, as a result of that first reading with Ross, and things I learned since, I have come to *know* that reincarnation is true. One intuits such a thing. I can't prove it to anyone else, nor have I any desire to. But I *know*. And this knowing began with the things Ross told me in that first reading about my past lives. There was a sense of fitness about them.

"One very odd thing occurred when Ross described one

of my purported incarnations which fell in the era in which my great-grandparents lived.

"He said, 'Thou wast the one who directed operations of the planting of crops by many around the area of Baltimore,' which I took to mean that I was a plantation overseer.

"But he added, 'On the Lord's Day thou wast a man of the cloth. Thy name was Hans Jordan.'

"I sat bolt upright as if someone had stuck a pin in me. *Jordan* was my great-grandparents' name! The last time I recall hearing it mentioned was when I was fourteen or fifteen. And here it was, coming out of the mouth of a psychic.

"The significance of this I'm not sure of, but certainly Jordan is not Smith or Jones. It's an unlikely name for Ross to come up with. Maybe there was some familial link with my great-grandparents in that prior life, for it seems, as a rule, that we have been close in previous incarnations to people who are important to us.

"Ross said that I was a hellfire and damnation preacher and had 'lost' karmically because of that. He also said that in reaction against my religious excesses in that prior life, I had no interest whatsoever in organized religion in this life. And that is perfectly true. Spiritual values have always been important to me but theologies and church institutions have seemed to me man-made and very arbitrary, in the same way that different psychoanalytic systems are human creations and can be quite arbitrary."

Logan Stanfield left that first encounter with the slumbering seer in an intellectual and emotional tumult. There was excitement. Curiosity. Wonderment. And a need to know more, to probe deeper.

Dr. Stanfield returned for a medical reading. And this was quite evidential. Basically, Peterson gave him a clean bill of health. However, he mentioned some "lesions" in the gastrointestinal tract which had healed, causing no trouble.

"The fact is," said the psychoanalyst, "that some time before this an internist had done on me a GI series, as we doctors call an examination of the gastrointestinal tract, and reported that I had diverticulosis.

"This is a condition in which the walls of the intestine, as it weakens with age, develop small outpockets. Unless these outpockets become inflamed (a disease which is called diverticulitis), the condition is asymptomatic, that is, symptom-free.

"However, I didn't like the idea of having diverticulosis, even if it didn't cause any symptoms, and I told myself, 'I will not stand for it. I'm going to use my mind to heal that condition.'

"Well, apparently I succeeded. Here Ross picked up healed lesions in my gastrointestinal tract, which I believe were the marks of my previous diverticulosis."

However, Peterson also mentioned another health fact about Logan Stanfield. The reading said that during the previous ten years he had had "respiratory problems" and "attacks of wheezing, quite severe at times."

Said Dr. Stanfield: "This was quite correct. I don't wheeze now, and I didn't at the reading with Ross. But as a matter of fact, one of the reasons I left New York City and came to Toronto was to escape the highly contaminated air in Manhattan. From breathing that pollution I had frequent attacks of wheezing and actually developed a condition bordering on asthma. So Ross was quite accurate again."

When Logan Stanfield told his wife-to-be about the uncanny man with the virtually all-seeing eyes, she asked for a reading. And she received her own peculiarly convincing evidence that there was something to this psychic business.

She asked the entranced Peterson to locate the form of

a close friend and gave his name and address, in a city in the western United States, about 2,000 miles from where they were. Peterson had trouble finding the friend. He said that the form was not home. The address of his place of employment was given but Peterson said that the form wasn't there either.

"Unless it be one fair of hair," the entranced psychic said.

Assured that this was the wrong person, Peterson said he would continue searching. His eyeballs were racing back and forth like crazy under the closed lids.

Finally, the seer said: "Though the form is at neither of these locations we have the pattern and vibrations of his mind."

Logan Stanfield, who was present for the reading, was once again struck by a sense of the utter incredibility, in commonsense terms, of what they were experiencing.

"It was," he said, "as though a television camera had been sent out on a space vehicle, had hung suspended over a location, scanned it and determined that the individual being tracked was not there in terms of the dense physical body and yet picked up the waves emanating from his brain and flashed an image of him on the screen back at the base."

When Peterson did get a fix on the friend and began describing him, there was no doubt that the psychic had the correct person.

"He spoke of his emotional state, which was negative, and of the great conflicts he had in relations with women," said Logan Stanfield. "He described him very accurately.

"And then he said something unexpected.

"'Ye will hear soon from this friend and he will be requesting that he spend a period of time with ye, for he is quite depressed.'

"Well, six weeks elapsed and sure enough a letter arrived from this friend notifying us that he was coming into Toronto on a certain flight, asking us to meet him at the airport, and volunteering the news that he was feeling quite depressed."

Psychics, like physicians, tend to specialize; to be more competent in certain areas than others. One would not normally ask an obstetrician to perform brain surgery or a brain surgeon to remove a diseased kidney. So, people with psychic gifts tend to exercise them in particular directions.

One, for example, may be exceptionally good at *psychometry* (picking up information by handling an object), while another majors in *precognition* (flashes of the future) and still another has a notable facility for coming up with obscure names from an individual's past.

Since Ross Peterson consciously modeled himself on Edgar Cayce it is not surprising that his major psychic talent should be *medical* clairvoyance.

This is a talent which lends itself readily to verification. If the psychic says there is a tumor at a certain site in the body, tests can determine if indeed it is or is not there. This kind of verification is what built Edgar Cayce's reputation as a psychic. Without the evidential character of his *medical* readings, it is doubtful whether much attention would have been paid to his much less verifiable readings on reincarnation and Atlantis. It was the medical readings, with their high level of accuracy (though, to be sure, Cayce had his share of 180-degree misses too), which stamped him as a genuine seer. And so it is with this latter-day Cayce, Ross Peterson.

Dr. Logan Stanfield's estimate that out of the fifty medical readings he has followed up, Peterson was accurate nine times out of ten is adequate to rule out coincidence or guesswork as explanations. Such a string of coincidences would be comparable to someone tossing a coin and regularly coming up with heads ninety times out of a hundred. As pure chance this would be more astounding than ESP.

What about fraud?

Well, since Peterson, in the vast majority of cases, has never seen the subject before (and in some cases was not even told his name beforehand) prior research seems less than likely, to put it mildly.

The notion that Ross Peterson somehow bones up on the cases in advance is stretching credibility to its outermost limits, and beyond. Has he also memorized textbooks on anatomy, internal medicine, and neurology? One medical person said: "He talks as if he had taken an eight-year college course!"

Also, he often detects diseases of which the patient and his doctor are unaware. How could Peterson research information not yet known?

Then, too, he sometimes picks up *incipient* conditions too subtle, apparently, for orthodox medical tests to detect.

"From my multiple contacts with the readings," said Logan Stanfield, "I've come to believe quite strongly that when Peterson apparently misdiagnoses a condition he may, in some cases, actually be *anticipating* the condition before it becomes clinically manifested.

"His psychic sensitivity to subtle malfunction in any part of the body may be greater than that of any standard test we've got in medicine."

An example: In one case Peterson described a woman as "having used measures to prevent conception which are very detrimental to this body, having caused imbalances within the body."

The reading went on to say that the woman felt "a tingling, a numbness, in the left leg." She confirmed to Dr. Stanfield that this was true, though she hadn't spoken to anybody about it because it seemed so trivial.

The reading added: "This entity has suffered headaches at times that would almost cause blindness."

The woman was suffering headaches at the time. But
note the phrasing: *that would almost cause blindness.* It
is striking in the light of subsequent events.

"This woman was taking an oral contraceptive prescribed by another physician," said Dr. Stanfield.

"Several months after the reading she had what we
commonly call little strokes. This means that arterioles,
smaller branches of the arteries in the brain, become
plugged. The woman complained of an intensifying of her
headaches and a blurring of vision. In fact, she came back
from holidays with what proved to be unilateral quadran-
tal hemianopsia, which is blindness in a certain part of
the visual field in one eye due to some pathway in the
brain along which the visual impulses travel being oblit-
erated by a lesion of some kind.

"Immediately I referred her for a thorough medical
work-up and the diagnosis confirmed that she had cere-
bral vascular insufficiency with a visual loss.

"The Pill was undoubtedly the cause and its use was
immediately stopped.

"In this case, Ross appears to have sensed a condition
several months before it became clinically evident."

In another case, said Dr. Stanfield, a woman was said in
a reading to have "a tendency toward diabetes. This
should be watched . . ."

At the time tests failed to confirm Peterson's statement.

"However," added the psychoanalyst, "two years later,
this woman, with whom I was still in touch, began
developing certain problems, such as recurrent yeast infections. She took a glucose tolerance test and it showed a
tendency toward diabetes. She was spilling sugar into her
urine but only after she had ingested large amounts of
carbohydrates.

"So Ross was right. The *tendency*—for that's precisely what it is—to diabetes is there, in this woman's body.

"I think Ross picked up this incipient condition at a stage when classical medical procedures were just not sensitive enough to detect it."

One wonders how much Peterson's margin of error would be reduced if two-year follow-ups could be made of all the subjects for whom he gave readings. How many of those who were told they had a "tendency" to hyperthyroidism, or hypothyroidism, or hypertension, or any one of a dozen other things, would report that the condition, undetectable at the time of the reading, had since shown up?

In some cases, Peterson correctly distinguishes between diseases or symptoms which are psychosomatic or organic, and those which are purely imaginary.

One reading told a woman: "If the mind is filled with thoughts of sickness, sickness, sickness, and the fear of the same, the entity feels sick though no actual physical condition exists . . . This one has had the hands of the faith healer laid on, has sought out numerous medical doctors, has sought members of all varieties of the healing arts, yet no relief has been found . . .

"The mentality of the hypochondriac is evident in this one. . . ."

Dr. Stanfield commented: "I can confirm, though Ross did not know this woman at all, that her constant stream of talk and of thought is about illnesses. Vague, ill-defined disorders or imagined conditions within her body. This woman may well be the most severe hypochondriac that I have encountered in my twenty-two years of the practice of medicine.

"I have also found that her hypochondria is an exploitive method by which she manipulates people. She uses her imaginary illnesses to get her own way.

"Also, as Ross said in the reading, her history was

replete with healers, orthodox and unorthodox, of every conceivable sort and description. The reading was very accurate in sizing her up."

Like Edgar Cayce, his spiritual mentor, Ross Peterson stresses in the medical readings the crucial importance of spinal misalignments to normal health. The readings often recommend the corrective services of an osteopath or chiropractor.

Osteopathic and chiropractic theory says that *subluxations* (compression of adjacent vertebrae) and *rotations* (angular displacement or tilting of vertebrae) cause nerve irritation and muscle spasm and impair the "energy flow" to various parts of the body, producing symptoms which can range from violent headaches and irregular menstruation to increased susceptibility to infections of all kinds.

A chiropractor to whom Dr. Logan Stanfield referred a number of patients on the basis of the readings is Dr. William Zwarick of Toronto.

He said that he found Ross Peterson's descriptions of spinal misalignments "so minutely detailed and accurate that they sound to me like a report from another chiropractor. The man is incredible. It's as though he were X-raying the spine with his eyes, even when the patient is hundreds of miles away."

There was one peculiar detail about the readings which confused Dr. Zwarick for a time.

"When chiropractors speak of a vertebral rotation we mean that, if you divided the vertebra into equal halves, a rotation to the *left* would cause that vertebra in the X-ray to extend further to the left of center than it should. A rotation to the *right* would involve the opposite.

"Now, curiously enough, Peterson consistently speaks of what I would call a rotation to the left as one to the right, and vice versa. Because he's *consistent* in this usage I knew it wasn't simply a mistake. Finally, I figured out what it means.

"I realized that we chiropractors look at the spine from a posterior view, through the back. Apparently Ross Peterson looks at the spine from an anterior view. It's as though the body were lying face up and he looks through the body at the spine.

"Now, of course, a rotation to the *left*, as seen from the back, is a rotation to the *right*, seen from the front. This is just another incredible thing about these Peterson readings. And it tends to support the idea that he actually does inspect the physical form."

Let us look at some actual cases from Dr. Zwarick's files.

A young woman suffered from severe, chronic migraine-like headaches. In his reading, Peterson said: "The lack of a proper energy flow through the nervous system has caused this entity to experience excessive pain in the cranium—a devastating headache, so to speak . . .

"Now, in the birthing process of this entity there was difficulty experienced indeed, to the point where force was applied to help the delivery of the infant. In this process there was a mild separation, a pulling apart, of the cranium and the upper portion of the spine . . . The distance between the sphenoid bone and the atlas is greater than it should be. This distance should be lessened approximately eight millimeters, see?

"The chiropractor or osteopath should begin manipulations at the sixth cervical vertebra, working up to the third cervical, see?

"We feel that it would require at least twenty-six treatments here to completely correct the condition."

Dr. Zwarick's comments:

"Ross Peterson is almost 99 per cent accurate in this case.

"His knowledge of the spinal column is amazing. He

uses correctly terms such as 'sphenoid bone' and 'atlas.'
He talks, in fact, exactly as though he were a trained chiropractor or osteopath.

"Now, in this case there *was* a spreading apart of the
sphenoid bone and the atlas. He suggested the distance
should be lessened approximately eight millimeters. Actually, I lessened it approximately thirteen millimeters.

"He was correct in pinpointing the area between the
third and sixth cervical vertebrae as being misaligned.
And to top it off, he was almost exactly right about the
number of treatments it would take to correct the condition. He said twenty-six and there were actually twenty-
four!"

This particular case yielded another confirmatory detail. Peterson had recommended, besides spinal adjustments, the use of "massage, kneading the flesh, with the
tips of both fingers centered upon the vertebrae and moving in an upward and outward fanlike motion."

Said Dr. Zwarick: "Normally I would not have used
massage or any similar technique on a patient of this
type, but I took note of Peterson's suggestion and put the
patient on a physiotherapy unit called a sine wave. This is
strictly a muscle-stimulating device similar in its effect to
vigorous massage.

"Generally, I use the sine wave stimulator in cases of
athletic injuries to try to banish the muscle spasm. But in
this case, as Peterson suggested, it definitely seemed to
augment the effectiveness of the spinal adjustments."

Another case from Dr. Zwarick's files:

A reading for a male patient said: "If thou lookest at
the spinal column, thou wilt find misalignment of certain
vertebrae which are causing pressure to exist upon the
parasympathetic nervous system. Examine the fourth,
fifth, sixth and seventh dorsal and thou wilt find a certain
degree of subluxation and rotation to the left of these vertebrae.

"Now, this is directly affecting the free flow of energy throughout the nervous system and is responsible to a degree for a sensitivity evidenced within the liver . . .

"Now, there are further subluxations within the spine and thou wilt find these in the ninth, tenth, eleventh and twelfth dorsal, even into the first lumbar here. Now, the rotation here is to the left and is causing, again, a pinching, so to speak, or a lack of energy flow to the lower portion of the body . . ."

Dr. Zwarick commented:

"Peterson is right on here. X-rays confirmed the subluxations he described. The fifth, sixth, seventh and eighth dorsal vertebrae were suffering compression, as he said, and this is precisely the area that connects directly to the parasympathetic system affecting the liver.

"His pinpointing of the first lumbar vertebra further down the spine was also spot on.

"And again, where he speaks of rotation to the left, I call it rotation to the right. Never fails."

Another case described by Dr. Zwarick involved a woman with severe pain and excessive bleeding during menstruation.

The reading said: "In the lower portion of the spine, the third, fourth and fifth lumbar, there is subluxation. Rotation is to the right. This causes pressures upon the nerve endings leading to the reproductive organs. This entity has had problems relating to the menses."

Dr. Zwarick commented: "Again, Peterson is right on. There are subluxations which show up on the X-rays of the vertebrae cited—the third, fourth and fifth lumbar. And he's neurologically correct, for this is where the sympathetic nervous system comes into play with the ovarian function.

"And once again, he says rotation to the right while I say to the left. It's the craziest thing!"

What is Dr. Zwarick's overall assessment of Ross Peterson's spinal delineations?

"He is 95 per cent right, and perhaps that proportion is even higher. In some cases he's been virtually 100 per cent correct.

"There is absolutely no way that this could be fakery or guesswork. When you consider that his readings require an intimate knowledge of twenty-seven to twenty-eight-odd movable segments in the spinal column, anatomical terms, plus the tie-ins with the sympathetic and parasympathetic nervous systems—well, there's too much there for anything but an expert knowledge to be at work. In Peterson's case, it's obviously a psychic knowledge.

"And what astounds me is the fluency of the readings. The words just pour out of him, without any stopping to take time to think. My specialty is the spinal column but I have to think, to ponder, at least briefly, before making some judgments. Peterson makes them in the snap of a finger.

"To be honest, I would have thought a man would need seven to eight years of schooling in anatomy, neurology, and osteopathy or chiropractic to be that fluent."

To return to a point raised earlier in this chapter: Ross Peterson sometimes makes clear-cut *mis*diagnoses. Why? What causes the margin of error in his readings?

Dr. Logan Stanfield suggests that changes in the central nervous system brought about by metabolic imbalances may adversely affect Peterson's psychic performances.

"I do know," the psychoanalyst said, "that in one very short period, Ross made a clear miss in diagnosing a subject's physical condition and soon after, when I asked for a psychological reading on a subject, he came up with one that can only be called bizarre. It bore no relationship whatsoever, that I could see, to the facts of the case.

"Now, I discovered that in this period when his psychic

gifts were out of whack, so to speak, Ross was taking a very potent painkiller to deaden the abdominal cramps accompanying a serious stomach ulcer from which he was suffering. My feeling is that the painkiller, a synthetic narcotic, which he never should have taken, had disoriented him and produced the scrambled readings. The narcotic caused changes in the central nervous system which apparently disturbed the psychic function.

"Now we know that changes can occur within the central nervous system without drugs. Alterations in body metabolism, mood changes, stress—these all can affect the central nervous system. Therefore, it's plausible to assume that these can also affect Ross's psychic functioning.

"When he's in optimum condition—physically, emotionally, spiritually—the readings probably are at their purest and most lucid. When emotional or physical stress, overexertion or even dietary upsets adversely affect the central nervous system, the accuracy of the readings declines."

Dr. Stanfield remarked that over the two years he has known Ross Peterson he has observed a steady change for the better in his personality and general outlook on life.

"There were times when I was shocked by the contrast between the lofty level of the readings and Ross in the normal state. He could be crass, crude, rude. I think I once good-naturedly called him a Michigan Archie Bunker.

"But lately I have noticed a distinct mellowing. It's as though the influence of the readings is welling up from his unconscious and subtly remolding his conscious self. From him now I detect a kind of warm, spiritual emanation.

"I hope the transformation continues . . ."

Chapter Six

THE KARMIC BOOKKEEPER

The "law of karma," it has been said, is the law of the harvest.

"Whatsoever a man soweth," says the New Testament, "that shall he also reap."

The Ross Peterson readings, as did Edgar Cayce's, teach that the sowing and the reaping may occur in different earthly lifetimes. What the soul committed in a previous life determines its circumstances in this life.

This is the answer of reincarnation to the vexing question of human inequality.

Why is one man born a prince, the other a pauper?

Why is one born physically perfect and the other damned into the world with gross deformities?

"It is the law at work," say the Peterson readings. "Each entity reaps exactly what it has sown. The law is perfect. There are no mistakes, no excesses, no imbalances. It is just."

Thus far, investigation has failed to yield a case of alleged reincarnation from the readings which checks out in terms of proof that the previous personality actually existed. The problems in such investigations are enormous. Most of the previous incarnations are far back in history. Birth records, if they exist at all, are fragmentary and scattered. Place names change. Whole civilizations have come and gone without a trace.

However, this is not to say that there is no evidence in the Peterson readings to support reincarnation as a fact. The evidence is there but it does not take the form (as yet, at least) of documentary proof that the alleged previous personality existed at the time and place claimed. The evidence takes the form of a psychological quality which I call *resonance*.

The Peterson reincarnation readings almost invariably *resonate* for the person to whom they are given. They ring a bell. Somehow, the individual feels that the reading fits; that it captures qualities and nuances of his personality which are strikingly true, though often totally hidden to others, and explains them in terms of a karmic carry-over from previous lives.

Now, the skeptic about reincarnation can point out, quite correctly, that perhaps what's happening is that Peterson psychically picks up facts about the individual's hidden self and then casts them in the form of a previous-life fantasy. This would be remarkable ESP but not reincarnation.

Well, on this point the reader must decide for himself. One researcher, Dr. Logan Stanfield, said: "As a result of my readings with Ross I now believe in reincarnation. In fact, for me it's true beyond a doubt."

Here's some of the evidence from the readings. Judge for yourself.

A secondary school teacher was told that in a previous life he had been a parson in eighteenth-century Virginia. Before entering the ministry, he served aboard a slaving ship. He was so sickened by the cruelties he saw that he vehemently protested to the captain. For this insubordination, he was flogged.

"And that is why," said the reading, "thou dost bear even in this life the stripes across thy buttocks. And when anger at injustice rises in thee, the stripes become even clearer . . ."

Nonplussed, the teacher, who was not aware of any "stripes" on his buttocks, rushed home and asked his wife to investigate. A careful examination revealed that he did indeed have a series of very faint striations—"like faded scars from surgery many years after"—across his buttocks.

Subsequent observation has revealed, too, that when he is flushed with anger (and he often is angered by social injustice, among other things) the faint, white markings, so similar to scars from a whipping, stand out in bold relief against the reddened skin around them.

Now the conundrum: Did Peterson correctly divine that this man underwent a flogging in a previous life? Or did he clairvoyantly discern the idiosyncratic markings on the man's buttocks and around this fact weave, unconsciously, an elaborate reincarnational fantasy?

The question would be resolved, conceivably, if incontestable evidence of the existence of the claimed previous personality could be found. But research into that possibility got lost, as is usually the case, in a maze of inquiries that seemed to lead nowhere. Someday, the schoolteacher may come up with definitive evidence that a parson with the name Peterson cited did indeed live in eighteenth-century Virginia. But today such evidence is lacking.

Still . . .

A case of alleged reincarnation in which there was resonance for the subject was that of clinical psychologist Dr. Lee Pulos.

"In my immediate past life, Ross picked up a situation in which I was purportedly a half-breed—half Caucasian, half Indian—in nineteenth-century America, and this created incredible conflict and an identity crisis in me.

"Well, psychologically that fit. In my early life, as a Greek kid growing up in Calgary, Alberta, I went through an incredible amount of prejudice and rejection. I used to get in fights every week because I was Greek. And it took me a long time to work through the conflicts and identity problems that my situation created. It is as though my present life were a replay of the previous one."

Dr. Pulos added that in a still earlier incarnation, according to the reading, he and his present wife were married to each other and in this current lifetime were working on problems which had been carried over unresolved from that previous marital situation.

"Ross picked up what my wife and I were working on then in our marriage and it corresponded to what we are certainly working on in our marriage this time."

Again: Reincarnation, or clairvoyance plus an unconscious reincarnational fantasy?

The psychological subtleties of the Peterson "life readings" (as the reincarnation ones are called) are often so striking that some skeptics find themselves almost believing in a previous life against their will.

In one case a sitter was told that in a former incarnation he had been "a Mongolian soothsayer to the great Khan" (presumably Genghis Khan) and that his overweening ambition had been his downfall.

Desiring to usurp the Khan's power, the soothsayer deliberately falsified an oracle and said that a day which was disastrous for battle (disastrous for the Khan, that is) was eminently favorable. Thus encouraged by his reliable soothsayer, the warlord went forth to battle and suffered a calamitous defeat. Unfortunately for the soothsayer, the Khan himself survived and returned, raging against the one whose false oracle had led to such undoing.

"For punishment," said the reading, "this entity was made to suffer the most agonizing and lingering of deaths. He was suspended between two trees, his body stretched out by ropes, and bamboo shoots were allowed to grow through each of his kidneys."

Then the reading added: "No wonder this one has suffered from kidney stones in this life."

The man had, in fact, suffered two exquisitely painful attacks of renal colic (kidney stones passing from the body). But what impressed him more was the fact that Peterson had correctly picked up a facet of himself known, if at all, only to his wife—a colossal, almost megalomaniacal ambition. A lust for absolute power. A passion to rule over others. This trait he kept well hidden.

Also, the man was an astrologer, a modern equivalent to the soothsayer who, as the reading put it, "shook the bones and sniffed the entrails."

Again, the dilemma: Penetrating clairvoyance masquerading as reincarnation, or the reflection of a true previous life?

"All I can say is that it fit," said the sitter.

(It is pertinent, too, though again proving nothing, that Genghis Khan was a sadist who particularly delighted in creating ingenious modes of cruel and lingering death for his enemies. This is a historical fact which I doubt Ross Peterson consciously knew.)

The life readings are full of rococo names and details. A young accountant was told that he had worked 15,000 years ago "on the giant crystal in Atlantis." (Cayce mentions this "giant crystal," which supposedly was a power source, possibly akin to a laser, and was at least partly responsible, like an uncontrolled nuclear reaction, for the cataclysm which befell Atlantis). A young woman was told that she had been a shepherd in Persia in the twelfth century and her name was "Krisfondo." A middle-aged woman of mystical bent was told that she had been a priestess-healer in ancient Egypt in "the Temple of Sacrifice."

Such exotica tend to incite incredulity. And yet the stubborn fact of a psychological resonance between the individual and his or her previous lives exists, however it be explained.

One reading came up with an image of God and why He lets the law of karma operate which has a strange and beautiful symmetry to it.

"If thou canst," said the reading, "imagine God as thine opponent in a chess game. This is the master chess player but one who is so loving that he has the deepest desire that thou shouldst win; yet so objective, that he is unwilling to overlook thy slightest error or mistake."

Peterson himself says: "The concept of reincarnation satisfies me because I can't conceive of God being jealous, hateful or judgmental.

"I *can* accept the idea that everything I have experienced in my life, or have not experienced, for good or for ill, is the end result of my own deeds or thoughts in a previous lifetime."

The life readings offer karmic explanations of virtually every form of disease or condition of man, and, again, there is often a striking symmetry, similar to the kind of symbolism psychoanalysts refer to as "organ language." Thus a rash is often caused by a person's "itching" to do something forbidden. The ulcer victim has something "eating" him. The sufferer from a chronic neck cramp lives with a mother-in-law who is "a pain in the neck."

This sort of psychosomatic correspondence resembles the so-called karmic correspondences mentioned in the readings.

For example, arthritis is said to be caused karmically by a carry-over of fossilized thinking from a previous life.

"If ye be stiff and unyielding in thought," say the readings, "ye shall be stiff and unyielding in body."

The readings say that arthritic people are judgmental. Though they may appear to be kindly, inwardly they are hypercritical of others.

Paralysis is said to be the result of the individual being "at odds with himself." He wants to be terribly, terribly good or terribly, terribly bad but is afraid to be either. Therefore, according to the readings, he is "powerless to move—paralyzed."

A man suffering from diabetic blindness was told that in a previous life he had exulted in putting out the eyes of others, and so, in this life, like a boomerang, *his* eyes had been put out.

Usually the hideous diseases are said to be the result of the sufferer having relished the sufferings of others in a previous life. A man who had been disfigured by a series of surgical operations because of lymph cancer was told in a reading that he had been the keeper of a leper colony in a past life and it was his responsibility to feed the lepers, who were kept isolated from the rest of society. However, he diverted the money he received to buy food for the lepers to his own use and allowed his charges to starve to death, walled up within a giant stockade.

How do people react when they are told in a Peterson reading that their present plight is the result of their own deeds or attitudes in a former life?

Peterson says: "Ninety-nine times out of a hundred— and I've given about a thousand readings—the person relates to the reading instantly and feels comfortable with it. He or she feels that if this is something they *deserve*, then they can live with it.

"But the readings say that in most cases they don't have to just live with it. There is another course. They can be healed. And of course that's why the readings offer the prescriptions and various forms of treatment that they do.

"In other words, just because something is karmic doesn't mean that you're stuck with it. You *may* be stuck with it, but not necessarily and not in most cases."

The readings offer karmic causes for a variety of sexual conditions.

Nymphomania in the female, or satyriasis in the male (pathologically excessive sexual desire) is said to be the result of repressive abstinence and denial of the body in a previous life, coupled with a very judgmental attitude toward others who fell into the sins of the flesh. It's like the pendulum which, when pushed to the extreme in one direction, swings back just as far in the other direction.

Sexual impotence or frigidity also are linked to an overly judgmental attitude in a previous life toward those guilty of sexual misbehavior. Sometimes, there is a so-called primary cause rooted in a past life, and a secondary cause rooted in some trauma in this present life.

Thus a twenty-eight-year-old married man, athletic in appearance, came for a reading and asked directly: "What is the cause of my impotence and is there a cure?"

The reading told him that in his case there was both a primary and a secondary cause. The secondary cause was an incident in his childhood, when he was six years old, and was caught with a little girl indulging in some mutual exploration of their bodies. He was caught by some of his friends, boys his own age, who were angry with him because he had taken the girl into their clubhouse and the clubhouse was strictly off limits to girls. For this reason, his friends kicked him out of the club and stoned him—literally threw stones at him—as he fled home crying.

At first, the young man said that this incident was meaningless to him. But then, slowly, agonizingly, it came back to him. It *had* happened to him and he had repressed it, buried it deep in his subconscious, where it fostered a morbid fear of sexual experience because it makes one an outcast.

The reading said that the primary, or karmic cause of his impotence was the fact that he had lived in Old Testament times and derived a special delight from stoning to death women taken in adultery.

In this particular case, the reading recommended innovative sexual techniques—including "oral stimulation" by his wife—to overcome the impotence. And the young man later reported that the condition had indeed cleared up.

Another condition which may have both a primary and secondary cause, according to the readings, is a speech impediment, such as stammering or stuttering. The readings generally say that the victim of a speech impediment is one who suppressed the speech of others in a past life, refused to let others have their rightful say.

The secondary cause—the this-life cause—of stuttering, as described by the readings, is in harmony with modern psychology. The stutterer, say the readings (and many speech pathologists) is generally one who has been trained to stutter, usually by an overly concerned or dominant parent. The normal stammerings of very young children are magnified by parents who pay too much attention to them and thus unwittingly turn them into permanent habit patterns.

Congenital mental retardation is said to be the result of the victim having suppressed the gathering of knowledge by others in a previous life. A book-burning fanatic might return as a moron.

What the readings teach is perfect equity. As you were,

so you are now. And of course this applies to "good" karma as well as "bad."

The readings warn against any self-righteous or holier-than-thou attitude by those who have been spared life's major griefs. To fail to show compassion to any suffering human being, say the readings, is simply to store up for yourself bad karma. The high caste Brahman who lords it over the lowly untouchable is doomed to return as an untouchable!

One of the subjects about which the readings offer an interesting twist is homosexuality. To begin with, Peterson's trance utterances declare that with homosexuality, as with any form of sexuality, the only rule is: "If there is love, there is no sin." Whether the sexual behavior is male–female, male–male, or female–female is a matter of moral indifference, say the readings. The only criterion is that love should motivate the sex act, not mere lust.

However, the readings distinguish between two forms of homosexuality, one expressing bad karma and the other expressing what might be called neutral karma, involving neither fault nor virtue.

Bad karma is indicated by the guilt-ridden, tormented kind of homosexual. In such cases, the readings say that generally the individual has been guilty of persecuting homosexuals in a previous life.

Neutral karma is indicated in cases where the homosexual feels perfectly natural about his or her homosexuality; that this is the way nature intended them to be, and they have no guilt.

In such cases, say the readings, the homosexuality is the result of a gender change from the previous life. A man who has behind him three lives as a woman will probably be homosexual because it seems "natural" to him to love men. The transitional lifetime is usually followed by incarnations in which the individual resumes heterosexuality.

"Reincarnation?" says Ross Peterson. "You can take it or leave it, according to your own best judgment. But I take it because it makes sense to me and apparently to many others."

Chapter Seven

THE SEER'S SUCCESSES:
SOME CASE HISTORIES

Those who seek out Ross Peterson's help obviously have an open mind about his psychic abilities and at least the hope that he can help them—otherwise they wouldn't bother consulting him—but all are not, by any means, absolute believers.

One young man, in a reading given in March 1974 in Toronto, began by bluntly saying to the entranced seer: "I would like some evidence of your ability before I go any further. Tell me something about myself that others may not know."

Peterson did not take umbrage at the sitter for his candor; nor did he hedge. He merely said: "We will inspect things in thy past which others may not be aware of.

"If thou wouldst reflect in thy memory, during thine adolescent years, at the age of fourteen, thou wast engaged in a combative sport with others and there was an injury to the right arm, the elbow, and also the wrist.

"We will inspect other avenues of the past. In the second year of thy marriage there was infidelity practiced by thee for a short time, but thou art carrying it on still in thy mind even now.

"If thou wouldst again reflect upon thine adolescent years, thou disavowed any association between thyself and thy parents and left their home. But this was temporary and thou didst return."

Then the entranced Peterson said, almost wryly: "We will seek further if thou dost wish it."

"No, thank you," responded the sitter immediately. "I'm convinced! Now, may I ask you some questions about things that are troubling me at this time . . . ?"

Peterson has spooked many people out of their initial skepticism. In one reading a man asked if Peterson could locate the form of a certain young lady who resided at . . .

"Is the one extremely fair of hair? Golden even by nature?" interjected Peterson.

"Why, yes," the man replied in a startled voice, "but how did you . . . ?"

"The image of this one is very vivid in thy mind," the entranced psychic calmly explained.

Ross Peterson is used to receiving letters such as this, written by a woman in Ottawa, Ontario, dated March 14, 1975:

"Dear Mr. Peterson,

"I was deeply moved and humbled by the reading you gave me on February 25th. I have never received so accurate an analysis of my character and the areas in which I need to improve. I will earnestly try to change myself in the ways that I know—far more clearly now, thanks to you—are needed."

A book editor, Ann Stevens, had a reading with Ross Peterson on March 25, 1975, in Indianapolis. As a highly literate woman, interested in politics, civil liberties and other social issues, her reading, and her subsequent comments on it, are very significant.

"There is a mannishness about thee," the reading said. "Not in thy physical appearance but in thy thoughts, thine aspirations, thy desire to accomplish, see?"

The sitter's comment: "Yes, I recognize the Chinese concept of the yin and yang; the masculine and female principles; the active and the passive. And I am both. Most people do not see this in themselves, perhaps, but I do."

The sitter mentioned a particular house at a particular address and said that six people, male and female, were planning to live there in "a communal life-style." Would it work?

"No," said the reading. "It will not work. It will not work unless there are commitments by each to each, and a harmony created by like minds attracted together. This experiment is doomed to fail. However, there are lessons which could be gathered . . ."

The sitter's comment: "He was so right! It didn't work at all. Monogamy won out."

The reading stated that in a previous incarnation, the woman had been "one of those Christians who traversed from their country to other countries to subdue the heathen. In that part of the world which is now called Turkey there is even to this day an inscription on a stone under a tree of the olive indicating where thou wast interred. But are heathens, heathens? Only in the eyes of man. For in the eyes of God, all are Godlike, you see."

The sitter commented that the idea of her having been

"a crusader—a rather barbaric one" definitely rang a bell with her.

But the reading continued: "Thou art undoing in this life that evil which thou didst in the past life. Thou art tempted to help *all* who are aged and infirmed, oppressed and downtrodden. This lifetime is one of great gain for thee karmically. Thou hast turned away none from thy door, even though thou thyself often wast short of food. Thou turned none away. Color of skin means nothing to thee. And that is why those of the beautiful color have surrounded thee and will continue to do so."

The sitter commented: "I've been very active in civil rights and social justice and I've tried to live my principles. The reference to 'those of the beautiful color' I take to be my experiences in the South, where I lived with black people as a civil rights worker for several years, and also in the Chicago ghetto where I did the same."

The reading declared: "As to thy children, we have first the small female form. This was a difficult birthing process . . ."

"My daughter, my first child," commented the sitter, "did cause me much trouble at birth. It was a difficult delivery."

The reading went on: "The entity has a mild infection in the womb at this time. Nothing that is really serious but it is there . . ."

The sitter's comment: "I had this medically checked. It was true."

The reading described the woman's other child, "a small male form," and noted that from his earliest years he had been extremely active. "Do not let him play fourteen to sixteen hours at a time, as he would," the reading advised. "The child needs periods of rest during the day."

The sitter's comment: "My second child is a boy, he always has been extremely active, and as for the short periods of rest, even at age five he still naps frequently."

The following photographs are from the November 1974 interview of Ross Peterson by Allen Spraggett on "ESP—Extra-Special People," a series broadcast over the Global Television Network (Canada).

1. Author Allen Spraggett introduces Ross Peterson to his television audience as "an alleged second Edgar Cayce." The author's admitted skepticism at this point is obvious in the expression on his face.

2. Spraggett interviewing Peterson before the trance experiment begins. "What happens when you go into trance?" Peterson replied: "It's a form of deep hypnosis, actually, in which I become totally unconscious." "I've heard reports," said Spraggett, "that you do what Edgar Cayce did in the trance state—diagnose and prescribe clairvoyantly." "Well," replied Peterson, "I'd have to say that Cayce was the master and I consider myself pretty much a neophyte. But this is part of what I do."

3. The seer in a thoughtful pose, pondering one of Spraggett's questions. Dr. Logan Stanfield spoke, when first meeting Peterson, of "this tall, dark-complexioned, white-haired
man with silver flecks around the periphery of the irises of
his eyes."

4. The trance experiment in blind clairvoyant diagnosis is
about to begin. Irva David (later Mrs. Ross .Peterson) is
introduced as the "conductor"—the one who will induct the
seer into his trance state and give him instructions while he
is in it.

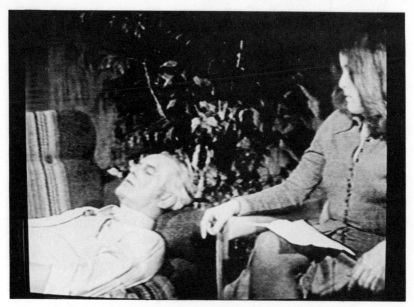

5. Peterson begins the deep breathing which induces the trance. Irva watches closely for the telltale signs that he has reached the deep level, at which point she, as conductor, will take over control of the seer's mind.

6. As the seer breathes in one nostril and out the other, the trance perceptibly deepens.

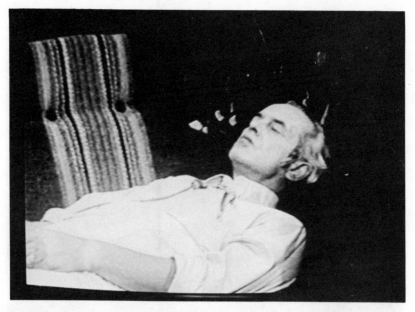

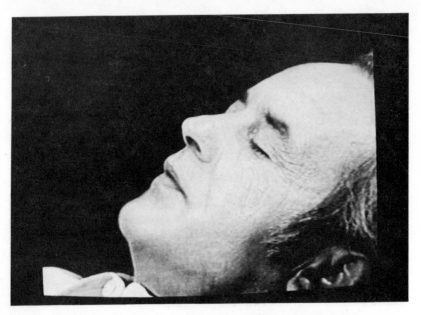

7. The seer has reached the deep trance level and the instructions are about to be given to him by the conductor.

8. "Would you please allow your mind to go to whom, to where, to what and to when it is directed," instructs the conductor. "Would you please locate the form of Mrs. X at such and such an address and notify us when you have located the same."

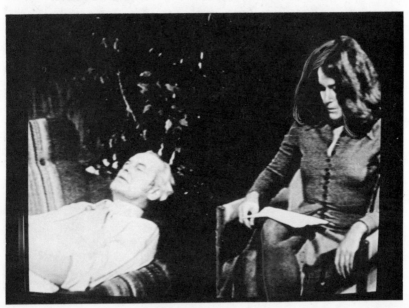

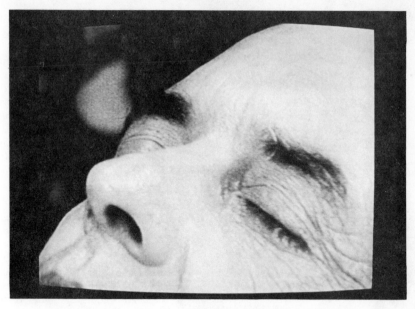

9. At this point the entranced seer's eyes begin darting back and forth under the closed lids, as though he were scanning a screen in his mind.

10. The entranced seer speaks, in a hollow, computerlike voice: "Yes, we have the form."

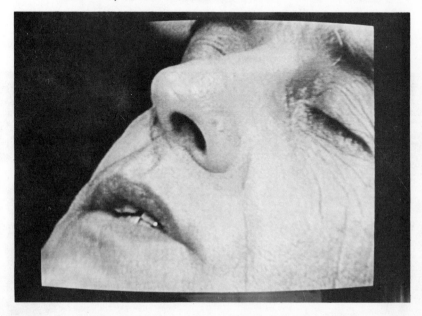

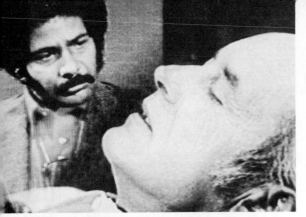

11. Dr. F. Logan Stanfield listens intently as the entranced seer begins describing the physician's mystery patient. "You will find in this entity, at the base of the cranium, on the left-hand side looking at the rear of the head, a degenerative process taking place that is organic in nature . . ."

12. Dr. Stanfield's expression is inscrutable as the seer concludes his detailed diagnosis: "This body is gravely ill . . ."

13. At the conductor's instructions, the seer begins to emerge from the trance. His arm, formerly totally inert, jerks to his chest in an almost spastic motion.

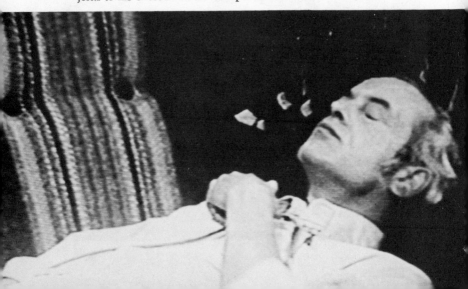

14. Dr. Stanfield evaluating Peterson's reading: "It was amazingly accurate . . . It's difficult to conceptualize just how such a power can exist but we have seen it demonstrated tonight."

15. The fully awake Peterson listens raptly as Dr. Stanfield enumerates his clairvoyant hits: "This patient is suffering from a disease . . . characterized by actual *organic* changes in the brain . . . This patient is indeed depressed . . . and is showing choreic movements . . ."

16. A look of quiet satisfaction on the seer's face as Spraggett asked Dr. Stanfield: "Could this diagnosis possibly have been a wildly lucky guess?" The psychoanalyst replied: "Impossible."

17. The program draws to a close as Spraggett, the erstwhile skeptic, sums up what Ross Peterson has just done and tells the television audience: "What we have just seen proves that Ross Peterson is a remarkable man who does remarkable things."

The reading concluded with an admonition and some dietary advice.

"An almond nut a day taken by this one," said the entranced Peterson, "will eliminate the possibility of a malignancy developing within the body. And there is great concern, a weight upon the mind, in this one about this particular disease."

The sitter commented: "I guess I was a cancerphobe. My father and father-in-law both died of cancer within a period of one month."

This brief summary of the reading has cited only highlights. There was an extensive excursion into the meaning of certain dreams the woman had been having, health advice, and references to her active sex life with a variety of partners ("So true," she commented), as well as other personal details. Yet Ross Peterson knew nothing about this woman, in the conscious state.

Asked to sum up her views about the reading, the sitter said: "I am convinced that what I experienced with Ross Peterson was the same process that is described in the readings of Edgar Cayce. What could be checked out, checked out. It was as though my mind, my life, was an open book to him. And I believe that the spiritual information he gave, about the meaning of life and the nature of God, was true.

"There was no denial of free will, no insistence upon the absolute fate of everything that occurs. Individuals and groups of individuals can shape the course of their destiny, the reading stressed, and it is the destiny of the human race to return to God.

"I believe this reading with Ross Peterson was a genuine experience reflecting other dimensions which exist alongside this familiar one of time and space. The Source communicating through Peterson was benign, and its desire was clearly to see us make benign choices—those

that would carry us toward God instead of toward self-destruction."

Another woman, Shirley Auburn, had a reading from Ross Peterson on February 14, 1974, in Bloomington, Indiana. Here is a summary of that reading and the sitter's subsequent comments:

"As we look in the colon we find a constriction which has existed for a number of years," the reading said. "This has caused discomfort in the act of elimination, of the disposal of feces from the body . . .

"If the diet is modified, this condition can be corrected without the need of the surgeon's knife. Prune juice should be taken daily by this one to allow more moisture to be absorbed into the intestinal tract and ease the constriction of the descending colon which causes an impaction of fecal matter. Corn oil should also be taken by this one daily. This one should be cautious in the eating of vegetables because the roughage would be abrasive to the sensitive tissue of the colon. Rather, the juices of the vegetables should be taken—especially of the cabbage and the carrot, two ounces of each mixed with one ounce of the corn oil and drunk at the beginning of each day. For breakfast, or at lunch, six to eight prunes, stewed, should be taken. These measures will eliminate the bowel problems."

The sitter's comment: "There had been a lifelong problem with severe constipation. The remedy given in the reading was followed and has brought complete relief. I am very thankful for this."

The reading continued: "The condition of the lower bowel is aggravated by a subluxation of the spine between the first and second lumbar vertebrae and also between the ninth, tenth and eleventh dorsal. There is also subluxation between the third, fourth, fifth and sixth cervical vertebrae of the upper portion of the spine and a rotation to the left. This causes pressures upon the sympa-

thetic and parasympathetic systems, cutting off circulation to the area of the cranium, thereby inducing the
ache that is felt, especially behind the left eye."

The sitter's comment: "I went to an osteopath and
X-rays confirmed the spinal misalignments mentioned in
the reading. Twelve or thirteen treatments were given
and there has been an over-all improvement in my
health."

The reading, speaking of prior lives, said that as a result of a lifetime of drudgery spent as an Indian squaw
skinning animals, "do not ask this one to remove the pelt
from the small animal and dress it, for this would be repulsive to her. It would even create terror in her, for that
lifetime was one of sheer drudgery."

The sitter's comment: "True. It would be totally repulsive to me!"

However, the reading said that as a result of a still
earlier life, in Florence, "when this one was the master
seamstress creating with the needle on the cloth harmonious designs of great beauty," she had retained "this same
ability in the present lifetime."

The sitter's comment: "Yes, I am a seamstress and
spend much of my time making lovely things."

The reading touched on the woman's divorce, noted
that she had long felt guilty about it, but reassured her
that it was caused as much, if not more, by her husband's
aggressiveness and overassertiveness as by her own failings. "He led thee by the nose, did he not? Did he not
command that thou cleanest the house! Did he not *command* that thou preparest the meal to suit him! Did he
not command, command, command . . . !"

The sitter's comment was: "Yes, my husband's attitude
was as described. But until the reading I had felt that
even though I was compelled to leave my husband I
had committed a terrible sin. I was haunted by the broken
marriage. This part of the reading brought immeasurable

comfort and assurance to me, and a truer understanding of what caused the disruption of the marriage."

The reading went on to note that though the woman had worried intensely about the effect of the marital breakup on her children, they had matured normally because "thou hast given them thy love."

The sitter commented: "There is a good rapport and much love between myself and the children."

On March 16, 1974, Mrs. Kay Albright of Spencer, Indiana, had a reading with Ross Peterson. Here is a summary of that reading and the sitter's comments:

"Regarding this entity's weight problem, if the body were to lie upon the floor, extending the feet slowly into the air pointing toward the ceiling, the body should repose upon the shoulders and the back of the neck with the hands upon the hips. Remain in this position for two or three minutes. Start thy day with it and it will bring about a better alignment of the intestinal tract. The intestinal tract is now too constricted and the food is held too long in the small intestine. This causes an *over*-assimilation of food and hence, obesity."

The sitter commented: "This exercise was tried for a month or two after the reading and was definitely, noticeably helpful. It was then neglected, alas, and has just recently been started again. It is a painful exercise but the result is a feeling of great relaxation."

The reading gave pointers on diet: "Precede each meal —and do not violate this—with at least two ounces of unsweetened grape juice mixed with the same quantity of lukewarm water. Taken fifteen to twenty minutes before ingesting any food, this will bring a better balance in the pancreas and the thyroid.

"In the evening meal—but only in the evening meal— one teaspoonful of pure olive oil should be taken before the grape juice. But only once a day for this particular body."

The reading went on to outline virtually a complete diet stressing the avoidance of refined sugars, the consumption of large quantities of yellow beans, squash, pumpkin, peaches, and garlic, and to restrict meat intake to fish, fowl or lamb. A daily intake of gelatin was prescribed too.

The sitter later reported: "All dietary information has been tried and is obviously helpful when followed. One of the most difficult things for me, since I am away from home much of the time, is the grape juice before each meal. However, I have noted that it is very effective, when used as suggested, as an appetite-satisfier."

The reading attributed a numbness in the sitter's arms and hands to "subluxation in the cervical area, in the upper portion of the spine."

Sitter's comment: "A chiropractor took X-rays and said my problem was in the upper portion of my spine. Treatments have eased the symptoms."

The reading said that the sitter would have the opportunity to move with her husband "to an area that will be more conducive to thy well-being, mentally, physically and spiritually."

"We did move," remarked the sitter, "but only a short distance from our previous home. Yet we have met people who have been a guiding light to us and the move has been good for us in every way."

The sitter simply asked about her son and if there were anything she could do to help him.

The reading noted a problem of bed-wetting and suggested as corrective therapy that the mother offer suggestions to her son in the sleeping state.

"When thy son is asleep, phrase thy suggestions, in a soft voice, saying that when the pressures that lead to urination occur the mind will immediately become aware of this and cause the entity to waken and go to the bathroom."

The sitter commented: "My son, at age fourteen, still had a bed-wetting problem. I gave the suggestion, as instructed by the reading, after he was asleep at night, following the wording in the reading exactly. And in only *two weeks* [italicized by the sitter] the problem was corrected. He no longer has the problem at all."

The reading noted that there were stresses in the sitter's marriage but declared that if "ye persevere, thy husband and thyself, both will be the winners. This marriage can be saved!"

The sitter commented: "My husband and I have both tried to follow the advice of the reading and we are winning! We later had a separate joint reading about our marriage and it gave the advice that 'the giving of love by one is always returned by the other.'"

The sitter was involved in three readings with Ross Peterson: this first one, a second for her husband separately, and the joint one attended by both in which marriage counsel was sought.

The sitter summed up her impressions of the three readings: "The joint reading was a very personal one. We asked if my husband should have the vasectomy he was contemplating and we were advised to go ahead with it, and that it would have a 'calming, tranquilizing effect' upon him. This has proved to be true.

"The three readings have been accurate. On a personal basis, my husband and I have used them to help us in our spiritual development. At the time of the reading about our marriage the union was virtually on the rocks and we were seriously considering divorce. Because of this reading we are now on solid ground and looking forward to many years together.

"The three readings have truly changed our lives. Happiness, which once seemed so elusive, now seems possible."

The woman's husband, Dennis Albright, in his personal

reading asked about two young men, naming them and giving their whereabouts.

Of the first, the entranced Peterson said: "Advice and counsel should be given to this young man—that the goods of other people *are* the goods of other people and his acquiring of these goods should be the result of what thou wouldst term honest effort, for there is some difficulty here. This one has light fingers and likes the material things of life . . ."

The sitter's comment: "He does have a problem in this area; he has been known to steal."

Of the second young man, Peterson said: "This one is the lazy bone. He does not like work in any form and will go to any lengths to avoid it."

The sitter commented: "He has been accused of this very thing by other members of his family."

Of a third young man inquired about, the reading said: "Thou wilt find that this one resents intrusions from any. This one will not accept pressure from any source, from anybody . . ."

The sitter's comment: "He is rather an introvert and does not readily open up. And he is *quietly* stubborn."

Could such a capturing of major personality traits in three individuals not known to Peterson be merely guesswork or coincidence? The sitter did not believe so.

"The aid received in these readings in response to questions about how to better understand others and myself and how to improve myself has been of tremendous comfort and guidance to me. I doubt if I could have come by the self-knowledge I've received in any other way," Mr. Albright said.

"The readings pointed out my weaknesses and also my strengths, enabling me to help myself. The insights received have been of immense value in my life-style, in knowing how to go about many things, how to deal with my wife and family, how to make a living—the whole spectrum of experience.

"Ross Peterson has developed these amazing capabilities and I don't know of any place in the world where one could receive this kind of information and guidance with such a great degree of accuracy."

Curt Friend, a businessman from Ottawa, Ontario, had a sitting with Ross Peterson in Toronto on September 27, 1975.

"It was a remarkable experience," Mr. Friend said.

"First, he picked up my physical condition exactly. He said that there were problems 'in the lower portion of the spine causing an imbalance to exist within the elimination system.'

"He was quite correct. I had recently suffered a slipped disk in my lower back which had impinged upon a nerve, damaging it, and as a result causing severe constipation.

"Then Peterson said, 'There has been a bone bruise on the tibia,' which of course is a bone in the leg. That was amazing because six months earlier, on a business trip to Japan arranged by the Canadian Government, I had made a misstep and fallen four feet, severely injuring my leg. The doctors said the bone was not broken but bruised, exactly as Peterson described.

"Peterson recommended chiropractic or osteopathic spinal adjustments for my back. However, he said there were three other health problems for which he wished to prescribe.

"One was the chronic constipation, the second was an hyperactive thyroid which he said was making me feel jittery, and the third was acute sinusitis.

"The treatments for the hyperactive thyroid and the constipation were combined. I was told to drink daily a large glass of prune juice to which had been added one drop of Lugall's Iodine Solution, which I got at a drugstore.

"For the sinusitis, the reading said, 'The sinus can be cleared here quite easily. Simply take a small receptacle, pour five ounces of peach brandy and to this add one half ounce . . . no, too much here . . . better to start it slow. Use one half teaspoonful of muriatic or hydrochloric acid mixed with the peach brandy. Then in the evening hours, before retiring, breathe in deeply the fumes emitted by this mixture. Do this once, then let the body rest from this therapy for nine days, then repeat it. The fifth or sixth application of the treatment should be sufficient. Thou wilt find that the eyes will water and thy nose will run and thou wilt spit phlegm which thou didst not think existed in thy body . . .'

"Well, I must say that the treatments worked. My jittery nerves settled down and the chronic sinusitis cleared up completely.

"There was one nonmedical detail in the reading which at the time was impossible to judge but which since has proven to be spectacularly accurate.

"I asked the entranced Peterson about an important business deal in which I seemed to be encountering obstacles.

"Peterson said that I would not be successful. The deal would go to another man.

"Then he added, 'But this one will pass on from a heart attack not long after the deal is settled.'

"Well, it's incredible but the prediction came true. I did lose the deal to another man, a fine person. But some six months later, on June 29, 1976, he suddenly died from a heart attack.

"I must say that Ross Peterson's reading impressed me enormously. Without having laid eyes on me before, he sized up my emotional state exactly, told me many things about my private life, and described people unknown to him but important to me with uncanny accuracy.

"I have no doubt that this man was tapping the same kind of Source that Edgar Cayce tapped."

In a reading given for Dr. Tony Kenworthy in Bloomington, Indiana, in March 1975, questions were asked by the sitter about his own health and that of a relative.

Speaking of the relative, Peterson said: "Tell him to look at his left hip. For there is a condition developing here that is going to cause him severe distress. It is the sponging effect of the bone. It might require the use of the surgeon's knife for the replacement of some of the bone . . ."

In his follow-up evaluation of the reading dated May 2, 1975, Dr. Kenworthy wrote: "I was particularly impressed by the accuracy of the medical part of the reading. The information concerning one of my relative's problems was particularly useful."

In a case I can vouch for, Peterson, in a reading, advised a woman who was addicted to cola drinks to wean herself from the habit by replacing the caffeine-containing beverage with a mildly stimulating tea brewed from the leaves of plantain.

"This is a common weed, trodden underfoot by many who know not its name. But this entity knows it by sight and it grows in profusion where she lives."

Well, Peterson was right about one thing: the woman for whom the reading was given, being an avid gardener, knew precisely what plantain looked like. But the second part seemed off base.

"I've never seen even one plantain growing around our place," the woman said.

However—and, again, here is one of the curious coincidences, if that's what they are, which so often are associated with the readings—within two weeks plantain began growing around the woman's home.

"Suddenly it's virtually everywhere I look," she said.

Now, in this case, was Peterson divining the future?

One never knows. But the fact is that, as the reading said, plantain "grows in profusion" where the woman lives, though it didn't at the time of the reading.

It is the *consistency* of Ross Peterson's results which are impressive. Psychic flashes come to many people. But Peterson is like a radio, which can be turned on virtually anytime and it works.

Of course, sometimes one gets the wrong station, or static distorts the reception but more often than not the message comes through loud and clear.

Chapter Eight

A PSYCHIC PHARMACOPOEIA
AND GUIDE TO GOOD HEALTH

In the thousand or more trance readings Ross Peterson has given, his unconscious mind, or higher self, or whatever the Source is, has come up with remedies for a wide variety of diseases and symptoms.

In some cases the implication is quite clear that the remedy is tailored to the individual and would not necessarily be effective for anyone else. In other cases, relatively few, the readings offer no remedy, simply declaring the condition irreversible. In many cases, however, it is suggested that the remedy, dietary prescription or exercises offered would benefit all who used them.

One thing should be made unequivocally clear: The

readings *never* downgrade medical science. In the hundreds I have pored over there is not so much as a suggestion of criticism of orthodox medicine. In many cases medical aid, such as surgery, has been recommended.

As a matter of fact, in Peterson's own case the readings urgently recommended surgery to correct an ulceration of his digestive tract. When Peterson (who is human, all too human in his aversion to hospitals) postponed the surgery, the readings reproved him. References to his own physical problem began obtruding into readings given for others. Ultimately, the readings *nagged* him into having the surgery. And, as predicted, it was an unqualified success.

The readings quoted have shown how often the services of the osteopath or chiropractor are recommended.

The remedies and dietary prescriptions set forth in the readings, then, are not to be considered a substitute for medicine or construed as an invitation to self-treatment of serious health problems. They are an adjunct, an auxiliary, a supplement, to standard medicine.

Certainly there is no evidence that anybody has been harmed, or could be, by the natural herbal remedies in the Peterson readings. On the contrary, there is evidence that many people have benefited from them.

The problem is, however (and I am very conscious of this and thus stress the point), that some overzealous individuals may be tempted to forsake standard medicine entirely and rely totally on the remedies given in the readings. This would be unwise and is not condoned by Ross Peterson.

In some situations, admittedly, orthodox medicine can do nothing. In such cases total reliance on the Peterson remedies poses no danger but offers the hope of a possible cure, or at least an amelioration of symptoms.

The general philosophy of health in the readings seems

sound, even by orthodox standards. The readings do not, for example, recommend vegetarianism.

"Man," one reading declared, "is neither herbivorous nor carnivorous but omnivorous. Therefore, eat ye meat for it builds the body."

The only meat more or less consistently proscribed is pork. Lamb, fish, fowl and, to a lesser extent, beef, are strongly recommended.

For those vegetarians who have ethical scruples about eating meat because it involves the killing of an animal, the readings suggest the "kosher" approach of Judaism.

"Say a prayer when thou dost take the life of the animal which is to be eaten. Or say a prayer of thanksgiving before partaking of the flesh of any animal.

"After all, vegetables too have awareness of a kind. If ye had ears to hear, ye could hear the cabbage shrieking when it is harvested. . . ."

The readings declare that in God's hierarchy of beings and values animals were intended to nourish man's physical life.

There is nothing faddish about the diets prescribed in the readings. They usually ban refined sugars, but this is in keeping with the growing opinion of medicine that modern man's enormous intake of such sweeteners has an adverse effect on health. The readings suggest natural sweets, such as honey, maple sugar or molasses.

The Peterson readings emphasize that underlying all healing is a proper mental attitude. Faith and love, say the readings, are healthful. Hate and fear cause damage to the body as well as the mind and soul.

"Mind is the builder," said one reading. "Mind is the master. Mind is the link to those creative forces of which we are all a part, see? And if the mind is filled with love, kindness and tranquillity then the body, which is merely an extension of the mind, must benefit, see?

"The body is made up of trillions and trillions of cells

and each has a form of consciousness. Yes, each cell. Each bodily cell must be considered as a world, as a universe, as a conscious entity in itself and it records all the stresses experienced by the individual.

"But at the same time that each cell is independent and unique, it is yet interrelated to all other cells of the body. And all are but an extension of mind.

"Mental attitude, then, can either build cells or tear them down, depending upon whether the attitude is positive or negative.

"That which is helpful in bringing healing to the body is an affirmation which should be repeated frequently and *believed.* 'If God be for me and with me, who or what can be against me?' Even as thou dost repeat this, *know* it to be true and healing will be accelerated. . . ."

This philosophy of the Peterson readings is quite consistent with modern medicine's growing recognition that much, if not all, disease is psychosomatic, the body being affected by the mind. To be sure, the relationship can be reversed in some cases in which *physical* disorders cause *mental* aberrations. But even in these cases, say the readings, the *ultimate* cause is wrong thought.

At a time when many researchers are exploring the possible correlations between even such a disease as cancer and personality, it would be imprudent for anyone to reject the readings' philosophy out of hand.

However, while postulating a mental or spiritual factor as basic to all disease, the readings recognize that in most cases practical remedies are needed besides a mental regeneration.

For the information of the reader, and for whatever value they may prove to have, here is a list of symptoms and diseases (arranged alphabetically) and the remedies the Peterson readings have suggested for each. In some instances more than one remedy is mentioned.

In using this list, the reader is counseled to follow his

own good judgment and common sense, which includes, presumably, regular medical checkups by his physician.

In assessing the value and usefulness of these herbal remedies, dietary prescriptions and exercises, remember the biblical test: "By their fruits [results] ye shall know them."

(Students of Edgar Cayce may note a similarity between some of the Peterson remedies and those given in the Cayce readings. Though Ross Peterson acknowledges that Cayce was his inspiration and spiritual mentor, he told me that he has not made an intensive study of that seer's remedies. I'm inclined to believe him. However, there is no doubt that he must have read some of them, even if only in a cursory way, and these would have registered in his mind. However, he denies conscious copying of Cayce.

(From the psychic standpoint, if Peterson and Cayce are tapping essentially the same Source—whatever that is —similarities in their remedies are to be expected. Truth, presumably, doesn't contradict itself. Not having studied Cayce deeply myself, I cannot judge to what extent Peterson's and his remedies overlap. But since Peterson has demonstrated unequivocal physic powers in diagnosis, character delineation and prediction, why should we not accept that he arrives at his remedies by the same route, while still allowing for a certain degree of unconscious absorption of Cayce material?)

ARTHRITIS

The readings advise spinal adjustments by an osteopath or chiropractor. They also recommend "the juice of the mustard green" and the "juice of turnip tops" to aid in removing from the blood toxins which lead to buildup of mineral deposits in the body's joints.

"An ounce to an ounce and a half daily of *either* of

these juices should be taken for a period of at least nine months." (Dramatic, sudden cures of arthritis are not promised.)

The readings also suggest gentle daily massage of "the center portion of the spine," or the affected joints, or both, with a substance composed of the following: one ounce of wintergreen, one ounce of spearmint, one ounce of eucalyptus oil and three ounces of peanut oil.

BACKACHE

The readings suggest an exercise to be performed daily, "slowly and easily, doing a little more each day.

"The exercise, which only requires a minute or two, is simply to stand erect, raise thy arms sideways extending to the horizon, slowly twist thy body so that the left hand comes down slowly and touches the right toe while the knees remain rigid. Then return to the upright position and do the same with the right hand to the left toe. Repeat this five or six times, slowly and easily. Only go down with the body to the point of discomfort, then stop. Gradually extend it each and every day."

The application of castor oil packs on the affected area of the back is also recommended.

"Once every fifth day, there should be the application of a castor oil pack shortly before retiring. This is to take four to six thicknesses of cloth and saturate it with as much castor oil as it will hold. Place it over the tender area and apply over it the heating pad as hot as the body can bear and leave it for forty to forty-five minutes. Then let the body rest. Twelve to fifteen applications of this should improve the back's condition."

An oil is also recommended for backache. It should be massaged gently into the skin over the sore area, "working in an upward and outward fanlike motion with the tips of both fingers." This should be done once a week for about forty to forty-five minutes. The formula for the oil, one part Russian white oil, three parts peanut oil and two parts castor oil.

BALDNESS OR PREMATURE HAIR LOSS

Several prescriptions are given to arrest, or reverse, premature hair loss.

One advises the ingestion daily of the following: "Combine the juice of the carrot with that of the natural juice of the peach, one or two ounces of each. Also mix a tea composed of two parts rose hip juice and one part ginger. Drink as much of this as the body can consume until the healing demonstrates itself fully. Then eliminate the ginger but continue with the rose hip juice."

An exercise is advised. "Simply let the head fall to the chest, rotating the head slowly to the left, to the back, to the right, then again to the chest. In a relaxed, loose, limp condition. Do this three times in the counterclockwise direction, then reverse the procedure and do it three times clockwise."

Massage of the area where the hair loss is being experienced is suggested. "Use either crude oil or Glovers Mange Cure. Knead it deeply and sharply into the scalp for a period of ten to twelve minutes. After the massage, apply a hot towel or hot pack to the area and let it remain for eight to twelve minutes. Then wash the area with a pure soap, preferably castile. Use this form of application of oil, massage and shampoo twice a week for a period of four weeks, then once a week for a period of two weeks. Then continue as is needed."

COLITIS

A three-day apple diet is suggested. "Eat the apple—preferably the Jonathan apple—and nothing but apples for three days. Consume large quantities of water too. This would enable a complete cleansing to take place of the digestive tract."

Cabbage juice is also recommended. "Not the cabbage itself, for the roughage would be harmful to the lower intestinal tract, but the juice of the cabbage, two ounces of it taken every other day for a period of thirty days."

DIABETES

The medical treatment for this condition is the daily intake of insulin.

However, in borderline cases, subclinical cases, in which tests show merely a "tendency" toward the disease, the readings suggest that its development can be forestalled by the inclusion of Jerusalem artichokes in the diet. Also recommended: "Consume one half-cup a day of tea made from the bark of the beechwood."

EYES: IMPAIRED VISION

In one reading, Peterson mentioned that the subject, a child, showed "a tendency toward weakness of the left eye." The child's mother confirmed that "his left eye turns when he is tired."

In this case, the readings attributed the visual weakness to subluxations of the third, fourth and fifth cervical vertebrae and suggested spinal adjustments.

In another case of impaired vision in a child, massage behind each ear was recommended.

"The massage should be done for only twenty to thirty seconds each night before retiring. In massaging there should be used the combination of one part oil of spearmint, one part eucalyptus oil, three parts castor oil. Rub a little behind each ear and this will be absorbed through the mastoid and eventually affect the eyesight."

In another case of poor vision, a simple exercise was recommended.

"Simply drop the head to the chest, letting all the muscles remain as relaxed as possible. Then rotate the head to the left, to the back, to the right, and again falling to the chest. There should be at least three full rotations counterclockwise, then reverse the direction for the same number of rotations. This should be done at least three or four times a day for ninety days.

"Then yoga should be practiced, particularly the skill of standing upon one's head."

HEPATITIS

In the wake of a severe viral inflammation of the liver, the readings suggested the following "to totally eliminate the virus and improve the liver's ability to remove toxins from the body.

"Seek out a physician and ask for quinine. The cleansing of the liver can take place gradually through the use of quinine.

"This could be prepared even by thyself. Take the bark of the quinine tree and pulverize it very fine. Then take no more than half a gram on a daily basis for the full cycle of the moon. [Approximately twenty-eight days.] Then stop for a full cycle of the moon. Then one eighth of a gram should be taken for a full cycle of the moon."

The readings also suggest that the liver's ability to detoxify itself and the rest of the body can be enhanced by the following:

"Take the juice of the leafy vegetable, spinach, chard or the cabbage. Any one of these or all three mixed. But only the juice. There should be at least an ounce a day sipped slowly at the beginning of each day, see?"

HYPERACTIVITY IN CHILDREN

The readings suggest: "In the evening hours give the child an ounce of good red wine diluted with an ounce of water. This should be given just before bedtime."

HYPERTENSION, OR HIGH BLOOD PRESSURE

"During the day, at least twice a week, a full eight ounces of blackberry tea should be consumed. The tea should be brewed from either the root or the leaf of the blackberry plant. Either is acceptable. Do not drink it quickly but sip it slowly. Take at least an hour to consume it. This gives it a chance to be fully assimilated by the body."

MOUTH PROBLEMS
(CHANCRES, SORES IN THE MOUTH, ETC.)

"Take the fresh leaf of the witch hazel," the readings suggest, "and hold it against the sore part of the mouth." This is also recommended in cases of inflammation of the gums.

THROAT PROBLEMS: MUCUS OR
CATARRH IN THE THROAT

A reading prescribed: "Brew a tea from the bark of the wild cherry, sip slowly during the day. It would do much to cut phlegm and mucus in the throat.

"Also, diet would be helpful. At least every other day eat three to six ounces of the leek, raw. It is important that it be raw. This will help eliminate catarrh in the throat or nasal passages."

THYROID PROBLEMS

1. HYPOACTIVE THYROID

The readings suggest: "Take cola syrup—not the cola drink but the pure cola syrup—and mix one-half ounce of the syrup with five ounces of water. Make certain that there is at least one glass of this consumed every day, preferably at the noon meal."

2. HYPERACTIVE THYROID

The readings suggest: "Take a 100-milligram kelp tablet once a day. Or take Lugall's Iodine Solution and add three drops only to a full glass of water. Consume this each and every morning until three cycles of the moon have passed (about three months). By then the thyroid should be back in balance."

ULCER OF THE STOMACH

"For ninety days drink no less than six to eight full ounces of the following brew: Steep a stick of the slippery elm, or the ground bark of the same, in hot water, making a tea. After steeping has taken place, the brew should be placed in a receptacle that will allow it to remain cool, not ice cold but cool. This should be the brew consumed each and every day for at least three full cycles of the moon."

VIRAL INFECTIONS

The readings suggest in any case of a viral infection, the following: "At least twice a day take at least six ounces made up of two ounces of carrot juice, two of cabbage juice and two of apple juice, preferably fresh, not canned. The cabbage used should be the green, not the white variety. And the apple used should be the Jonathan, McIntosh or Winesap, see?"

Now we come to an area where we must tread very cautiously: Suggested treatments for grave diseases. Cancer is one. Multiple sclerosis is another.

In cases of these diseases one hesitates to raise exaggerated hopes. Full advantage should be taken of the resources of medical science. What is given here, from the readings, must be considered hypothetical as yet (though the case of multiple sclerosis for which the particular treatment was prescribed has responded very favorably). These suggestions are offered for what they are worth.

In a case in which cancer had been arrested by standard medical treatment (radiation and chemotherapy), a reading proposed the following dietary additions "that will tend to be reductive of the rampaging growth of cells. Chew at least five full sprigs of parsley, raw, each day. It may be bitter to the taste so thou mayest blanch it lightly in a little butter. Also, the husk that surrounds the naturally dried almond fights the rampant growth of cells. Eat three in the morning, three in the afternoon, three in the evening, chewing them slowly."

In some places the readings have suggested at least one almond a day as a cancer preventive.

In the case of multiple sclerosis, the readings gave a treatment program that was complicated and extensive. Here it is in full. (As I mentioned, the sufferer, in this instance, has shown substantial improvement since following the treatment.)

"Spinal adjustments are needed here to improve energy flow to fight the virus which has invaded the sheath of the nerves. First of all, consider the upper portion of the spinal column: that of the atlas, the axis and the third and fourth cervical vertebrae. There is not only subluxation here but fusion.

"Beginning at the first dorsal, unto the ninth dorsal, there is subluxation with rotation to the left, causing pressures to exist on the lowest portion of the spine, the coccyx area.

"There should be the application of electrical energy flow throughout the body. There should be low-voltage application with one pole that is positive located at the base of the spine. The body should be a prone position lying upon the back. Apply the positive charge to the coccyx area of the spine. No more than two or three volts. That of a trickle of energy. The negative pole should be placed at the base of the cranium and the upper portion of the spine so that it touches the atlas.

"Allow the mechanical contrivance that is directing the energy flow to remain in place in the beginning no more than two to four minutes. This will excite the nervous system and eventually destroy the virus which has invaded the sheath of the nerves. The contrivance would have to be utilized for seven months and two weeks. Each time gradually increase by a small degree the amount of electricity which is allowed to flow through the spinal column. This will arrest the deterioration that is taking place within the central nervous system.

"Eventually the voltage should be increased to six or seven volts, which can comfortably be endured by this physical body. The treatment should be administered every *other* day, for there must be a period of rest after the application of the electrical energy flow.

"The application of colored light would be helpful to this body. The light should be infrared in nature and passed through a bright yellow filter. This light should be held eighteen to twenty-two inches from the body. Thou canst place the filter halfway between the light and the body. The body should be lying face down and the light directed at the base of the skull.

"Massage should be utilized just prior to the application of the light. There should be two forms of massage used. That in the upper part of the body, from the neck to the base of the brain, should utilize a mixture of one part oil of peppermint or spearmint, two parts peanut oil, three parts corn oil, four parts castor oil. Mix this together, then beginning at the third cervical, place the hands, but especially the thumbs, on the vertebra itself, moving the thumbs outward and upward towards the ears. Knead the side of the neck with the tips of the fingers. This massage should be carried out for six to eight minutes. Then the application of the infrared light through the yellow filter.

"A pack should be placed along the entire spinal column. Take a cloth, preferably flannel, of four to six thicknesses. This cloth should be long enough to extend from the base of the spine to the top. It should be six inches in width.

"After the application of the electrical energy flow, immerse this cloth in pure castor oil. As much as the cloth will absorb. Have the castor oil as hot as the body can stand. Place the cloth on the body, the length of the spine, and leave it from eighteen to twenty-two minutes. Upon removing the castor oil pack, more massage should be done. This should be from the top of the spine, gradually working down, using not the thumbs but the fingertips on the spine, kneading the flesh as the masseur would, pulling it downward, gently pulling it downward rubbing the castor oil in.

"Increase the amount of massage as you increase the amount of voltage, but do the massage daily.

"Halfway through the day this body should be given two ounces of cabbage and two ounces of carrots, preferably grown in the area where the body resides.

"Sweets taken should be honey or molasses, no other.

Figs or dates would be almost a spiritual food to this one. Only dark unrefined bread should be taken.

"Bananas should be avoided by this one. Pork should also be avoided. The body should have fish, fowl or lamb; baked, broiled or boiled. Never fried.

"Coffee would be helpful to this one because it would stimulate the nervous system. Tea brewed from rose hips would also be helpful to this one, but not ordinary tea, because there is too much tannin in it.

"This one's meals should be started with red wine—only the red—three quarters to one and a half ounces taken prior to the ingestion of food.

"Try to do yoga. It will be discouraging at first but thou wilt find thyself able to do a little more each day.

"Hold in your mind the picture of thyself strong and well."

An interesting sequel to this treatment for multiple sclerosis given by Peterson in August 1974 is a Reuters news dispatch from London dated July 7, 1976.

The dispatch reported that "electrical stimulation of the spinal cord of patients suffering from the crippling disease of multiple sclerosis has produced dramatic improvements, according to *Lancet*, Britain's prestigious medical journal."

The story said that the new treatment "is based on the theory that electrical charges can open up new nervous pathways around affected tissue . . . Two patients had tiny platinum electrodes implanted inside their spinal columns. These were attached to a device, carried by the patient, which delivered a series of electrical pulses every second. . . ."

This remarkable similarity between this new treatment and the one outlined by Ross Peterson in trance *Two years earlier* raises the question of whether Peterson's unconscious mind, like a psychic vacuum cleaner, sucks in medical data from all over the world. Two years ago the experimental treatment probably was at least an idea in the mind of some British researcher. Did Peterson tap this source?

Another similar case exists in which Peterson's clairvoyant prescription coincided with an experimental medical treatment of which he apparently could not have been consciously aware.

(On February 19, 1975, in Toronto, Peterson gave a reading for a seventeen-year-old boy who was dying from brain cancer. Already virtually half his brain had been removed in a desperate attempt to stop the rampant malignancy.

In the reading, Peterson, among other suggestions, prescribed an "heroic" treatment—the administering of arsenic. "Ye can start with as little as one eightieth of a gram in capsule form," the reading said, "and this should be gradually increased until this entity would be able to take into the body that which would normally cause the expiration of a healthy man, see?"

The reading suggested that the arsenic would destroy a repiratory virus which was attacking the boy's lungs, enabling his body to regain the strength to fight the cancer in his brain.

Treatment with the arsenic was begun but the boy died. Cause of death: acute respiratory infection, as Peterson had said.

Some six months after this reading an item appeared in the *National Enquirer* about "Red Chinese researchers who report remarkable success in using strychnine nitrate —a poison—to treat a deadly form of cancer . . . aplastic anemia."

Again, did these Chinese experiments, unreported in the West at the time of his reading, prompt Peterson's trance prescription of arsenic—like strychnine, a poison— for the case of brain cancer?

We simply do not know where Peterson's prescriptions come from but in these cases they appear to have anticipated or closely coincided with similar treatments devised by medical researchers in other countries.

Chapter Nine

THE INTERPRETER OF DREAMS

"Dreams," said Sigmund Freud, father of psychoanalysis, "are the royal road to the unconscious."

A dream is a message from yourself to yourself; from the deep, unconscious recesses of the mind to the level of conscious awareness.

In the past, dreams were considered visions from the gods, divine revelations, or messages from spirits (either good or bad, depending upon whether the dream was comforting or terrifying).

Whatever they believed about the source of dreams many ancient cultures were surpassingly wise in their interpretation. Moreover, some even practiced the *program-*

ming of dreams, an art which has been rediscovered only in modern times.

Hypnosis, for example, can be used to induce dreams. If the hypnotist says to the entranced subject, "You will have a dream tonight that will shed light on your problem and you will remember it vividly," the subject *has* such a dream and recalls it.

Now, hypnosis appears to have originated as "temple sleep" in ancient Egypt. The sick made pilgrimages to temples whose particular patron deities were known especially for their curative powers. The priests bade the sick pilgrim spend the night within the temple walls. He was told—no doubt by hypnotic suggestion—that during his sleep the god of the temple would appear to him in a vision and bring healing.

And, during the sleep, more often than not, the pilgrim did experience a visitation by the god in a vivid dream and awoke cured.

In the Old Testament, Joseph was famed for his skill as an interpreter of prophetic dreams. And in the New Testament, Pilate's wife is reported to have begged him not to have anything to do with killing "this just man," Jesus, about whom she had been "much troubled" in her dreams.

The emphasis on dreams continues in modern psychology. The psychoanalyst, especially, regards them as an invaluable means of uncovering hidden inner conflicts, tensions and strengths.

Ross Peterson appears to be a veritable wizard at interpreting dreams. And he strongly recommends that individuals learn the skill of recalling and decoding their own dreams. This skill, he says, can be an important step on the road to spiritual and psychic growth.

In his emphasis on the value of dream analysis for self-growth, Peterson is again echoing his mentor, Edgar

Cayce, who showed the same uncanny knack for unraveling the secrets of our somnambulistic scenarios.

Why are dreams cast in the form of symbols? Why are they not simple, direct communications from the unconscious mind? If it is so important that we receive these messages from ourselves to ourselves, why is the message so often hard to decode?

Well, the Peterson readings say that symbols are the native language of the unconscious mind. It expresses itself in symbols. They are to the unconscious what words are to speech.

Moreover, symbols serve to compress a rich diversity of meaning into a small compass (one symbol is worth a thousand words). And most important, dream symbols demand that we reflect upon them before their meaning becomes clear. Now, this process of reflection is a period of gradually increasing self-understanding. By the time we have come to realize what it is the dream is saying, we are prepared to accept it.

Some of the messages communicated by the deep mind would be traumatic on the conscious level if stated bluntly. The messages are veiled in symbols because the time and effort needed to strip away the veils enables us to grow psychologically strong enough that the dream's meaning is tolerable. Otherwise, it might destroy us.

"Thy dreams," said a Peterson reading, "will only give thee what thou canst bear at that time; not a wit more nor a wit less, see?"

According to the Peterson readings, dreams can take on a wider meaning than a message from our private unconscious mind. Sometimes they carry insights from the universal pool of consciousness, "that immortal sea" of wisdom which presumably is the Source of the readings.

"Many times in dreams," a reading declared, "the mind and soul of the entity leave the physical form and seek

out those levels of consciousness where needed knowledge is stored.

"The problem is that when there is the reuniting of the
body and soul, often what has been given by the larger
consciousness is forgotten.

"But there are no dreams that are idle, see? Thou hast
never known anything important in thy life that thou
didst not first dream of. Thou mayest not remember, yet
thou hast dreamt it nonetheless."

Here are some case histories of people who brought to
Ross Peterson dreams which they sensed were significant
but could not interpret. In trance, Peterson unravels them
in a manner which includes, even as it transcends, the insights of Freudianism.

"For dreams often relate to the soul-mind," said a reading, "and if psychology does not acknowledge this, its
dream interpretations will fall short of the whole truth."

One sitter was a young woman, from Los Angeles, in-
telligent, a political activist, and troubled by two dreams.

"Give us thy dreams," the entranced seer said.

There followed a fascinating *pas de deux* in which the
dreamer and the interpreter interacted in an intricate psychological choreography. Peterson was in perfect step
with the woman as she related her dreams. It was as
though he were inside the dream with her. See what I
mean . . .

The woman began describing the scene: "I dreamed I
was supposed to get a hotel room and a lawyer. This was
my mission. I stood in front of a hotel. It was night and
the lights inside were shining through the windows. It
was an old-fashioned hotel. There was a porch on the second floor that hung over, and it had very strong pil-
lars . . ."

"I see," interjected Peterson, "that in its entirety the
hotel had *three* stories . . . Yes . . . Continue."

The woman, obviously taken aback by this anticipation of what she had been about to say, faltered as she tried to resume the narration.

"We will give thee what has been given to thee," Peterson offered at this point. "We will carry thee through this dream as thou wilt carry us through it.

"First of all, the hotel represents that which is a temporary abode, does it not? As what thou art doing, or contemplating doing in that body of thine, at this time, will prove to be temporary.

"The mission to see one who is an authority in the interpretation of the law has a twofold meaning.

"First of all, what is the law? Who is the giver of the law? Art thou not really seeking him, see?

"The second import is that the law, and the interpretation and application of it, is important to thee at this time, and thou wouldst be proficient in such interpretation and application, see?

"The second floor of the hotel in thy dream signifies that which is known as the subconscious. The first floor represents the conscious, physical existence. The second floor, where the entity seeks a room in the dream, is higher than the level of material existence. This means that the entity is seeking knowledge from the unconscious not available on the conscious level.

"The third floor of the hotel, which thou dost not reach in this dream, represents the superconscious; or the essence of Spirit itself; the creative forces which underlie all that is; the very Godhead.

"As to the lights in the hotel, they represent knowledge. In essence, all men are light, not darkness, for they derive from the Godhead, which is pure light . . .

"The columns in front of the hotel were four in number"—the woman, again obviously taken aback, allowed that this was so—"four, representing the four dimensions of man: fire, earth, air and water, symbolizing balance, see? Continue."

"Well," said the woman, her voice unsteady, "I went into the hotel but only when it was morning. I stayed outside all night and watched people go in. I only remember men, although there may have been women, I don't know . . ."

"This," interjected Peterson, "is because of that which is unresolved in thee. For thy difficulty is with the opposite sex, is it not?"

"Well . . . I feel a conflict about my femininity," the woman allowed.

"Anyway," she continued after a thoughtful pause, "I remember the man who was standing at the door. He was in his mid-fifties. It seemed he had gray hair and a grayish face. It was his job to take a person in and each time he said to a man who'd come to get a room there, would he like to have a nice young woman for the night? And then they would go in.

"By morning the sun was shining and I went to the door. This man treated me the same way. He said the same thing to me and I said, 'I know you're tired but have you *looked* at me?' He did not answer, so I said, 'Well, if you're going to do this for me, please wait until tonight,' and he did not answer.

"I followed him inside and to the side of the building through the doorway . . ."

"To the *left* side of the building," Peterson interpolated in a matter-of-fact tone.

"Yes, yes—to the left side, that's right. Anyway, we went up a steep staircase that was like a service staircase. We got to the second floor and went through the door into a very pleasant lobby and he took me to the front of the building into a room—it seemed like more than one room—that opened onto a balcony. He was gone.

"I went and saw the balcony. Then I went back and

phoned Mildred Varonne, who is the woman I work for. I edit books for her."

Here Peterson cut in: "The importance of this dream, of this second portion, is simple indeed: Do not prostitute thy principles for anybody, see? For when thou goest to the second floor, representing the subconscious, it will show you what your inner source of power is, see? And turning to the left upon entering the building shows that this inner power should be applied to some problem in the physical side of thy life.

"Climbing the steep stairs shows the effort that must be applied to reach the source of power within.

"Now, in all *thy* dreams, whenever thou art utilizing the telephone, the newspaper or a book, it represents a message to *thyself*.

"So thou must ask thyself: How can I best interpret my phone call? The one whom thou didst telephone in thy dream—how dost thou feel about this one? For that person is only an extension of thy personality. And those traits which thou dost admire in this one are *thine* and thou wouldst keep them thine."

"Well," said the woman, verbally crinkling her brow, "she is in a position of authority over me . . . I'll have to think about it . . . Anyway, I told her that I had gotten this room. She approved and I hung up. I went back to the porch. It was breezy, pleasant, sunny . . ."

"What wilt thou find in the breeze?" Peterson asked. When the woman hesitated, he went on: "The breeze represents Spirit itself. The sun represents, again, the light. What is light? Light is energy. All is light. God is light, see?

"The light is shed on thee. The danger, as we see it, is that thou shouldst not prostitute thy principles on a temporary basis, regardless of that which thou mightst be tempted to call the circumstances.

"The law which figures in thy dream is the law given

by the Master—that ye reap what ye sow—and it is the whole law that applies to love. There are no injustices in this physical dimension. Not really. All of us are the end result of the law. And thou hast had this dream because thou art tempted to compromise thy principles in order to gain more contentment, shall we say?"

"Mmmm," murmured the woman. There was a reflective pause. Then she continued.

"There was a machine, or a wheel, or a large round mass. It was man-made. And it was dark . . ."

"It is the wheel of life," Peterson interjected, "and it is man-made. The number of spokes in that wheel, representing the number of lifetimes the entity will experience before returning to the Godhead, depends upon how each uses his power of choice, his *will*. For there is nothing stronger than the will.

"The wheel might contain as few as thirty lifetimes, or it might contain 360,000 lifetimes, depending upon how thou dost exercise thy will, thy power of choice. For this is a God-given gift to all, see?"

"Yes, yes," stammered the woman excitedly, "that's what it really was—my choice. I remember now thinking that while I was dreaming. And there were five men . . ."

"These five are thy guides," Peterson said. "If thou wouldst but call upon them, they would help thee find what thou needest at the time, see? They might be called angels by some. Their number, *five,* also indicates what is to be the quality of thy life—which is to be an adventurous one indeed, in the latter portion . . ."

"Well," said the woman, "I thought that one of the choices I had to make was to pick a lawyer, and from these five names—I don't remember what they were—I was to pick one. I decided none of them was my lawyer because my lawyer was a woman . . ."

"Thou didst not need to make a choice from those,"

said Peterson, "for thou art being told that that is part of thy personality. For that of the male represents the positive, does it not? And that of the female, the negative, does it not?

"There is a masculine quality about thee; not in thine appearance but in thy thoughts and feelings.

"We repeat: The message of this dream is that thou shouldst not allow others to lead thee away from thy principles; to cram concepts down thy throat which are not thine own."

"My other dream is more recent," the woman went on. "It had many parts. I was very startled by it all . . . I guess I was concerned about the relationship that I had in my dream."

"An extension of thy personality," Peterson interjected.

"Well, there was this woman that I know. She never really displays affection except to one man . . ."

"Dost thou find it offensive or pleasing?" Peterson asked.

"Well . . . I wish that she were more open to me. I really like her. In this dream I . . ."

"Thy subconscious is telling thee the same thing about thyself," Peterson said.

". . . well, she kissed me," the woman said in a so-there tone.

"Fine," said Peterson, "if thou dost like her. Thou art kissing thyself.

"One problem here is that thou art too concerned with what is called psychology. Now, psychology is good but not unless it recognizes the spiritual factor in man . . . Everything is not sexual. Everything is not a symbol of the genitals. Thou wouldst feel guilty indeed over kissing one of the same sex if carnal desires were involved but this kiss in the dream has nothing to do with thy sexual aspirations . . .

"Now, we are aware that thou hast spent two immediate past lifetimes as a man and so there would be certain women to whom thou wouldst be attracted. But thinking of it and consummating it are two different stories, are they not?

"These feelings are normal for *all*. Few would admit it. However, it is true, nonetheless. Thou art not sexually drawn to other women, in the true sense, believe us."

"And yet . . ." The woman faltered. "There is a woman that I think I love . . ."

"There is never any sin in love," Peterson declared. "But in thy case there would be sin in carnal love with another woman because this is not *thy* true nature. The feelings thou hast for this woman are fundamentally of the soul. The feelings she has for thee, however, may be carnal."

"Nevertheless," said the dreamer, "this other woman wants to live with me and she and I plan to live together with a man."

"It will fail," Peterson declared. "Thou wilt discover thy true sexual nature manifesting itself in jealousy over the man. Do not confuse soul love with fleshly love. What thou feelest for this woman is soul love."

To recapitulate in summary this rather lengthy dream narrative and interpretation: Peterson told this woman, who clearly had been troubled over her sexual identity and her occasional strong attractions to other women, that in *her* case these feelings were idealized expressions of a spiritual love and not manifestations of suppressed lesbianism. The experiment of living with the other woman (who may have taken the strong initiative) and the man in a sort of bisexual *ménage à trois*, would not work, said Peterson. The woman's true sexual preference —for men—would assert itself strongly. By entering into this experiment, the seer warned, she was compromising her own principles. This is what her unconscious mind was telling her.

The follow-up in this case is interesting. More than a year after the reading, the young woman wrote Ross Peterson to say that his prediction was accurate. The experiment in bisexual living had failed. Her heterosexuality won out.

Now, she said, she felt reassured about her basic sexuality and was comfortable knowing that the occasional strong attractions she felt for other women were symptoms of an ideal love, not sexual love.

The woman's preoccupation with questions of sexual identity showed up in her first dream, when she related how the man at the hotel had offered *her* a nice young woman for the night, just as he had the men. And her reply was significant: that she would accept the offer but not until that *night*.

This presumably indicated that sexual relations with a woman were associated in her unconscious mind with darkness, not light.

In her follow-up report, the young woman dwelt in considerable detail on Peterson's interpretation of the phone call to her employer in the dream. Peterson, you recall, had said that this older woman represented strengths which were also part of the dreamer's personality.

"At the time of the dream and the reading's interpretation," wrote the young woman, "I did not appreciate how much I did admire my employer and how many positive qualities, which I hope are also mine, I saw in her.

"This person committed suicide a year later and I was shaken and went back to the reading to recall exactly what had been said about her.

"The woman had retired and was very depressed. She

was alone in the world. Yet her accomplishments as a writer and editor had been great. She was a modest yet highly principled person who had worked for civil liberties, community theater, many community groups such as the League of Women Voters.

"Just before she died she had an aura of resignation and peace about her, as though she was ready to quit this life and go on to the next. She left instructions for her friends before she died, all very thoughtful, as she always was.

"She requested no memorials. Yet two weeks later fifty persons who had known or worked with her gathered in her honor and many testified to their beneficial experiences being with her."

In the dream, remember, this much admired woman had approved the room on the second floor—in other words, what the dreamer's unconscious was telling her to do—and this represented what the dreamer's best qualities also dictated.

This long, rather complex example of how Ross Peterson, in trance, unravels the tangled skein of dreams is typical. Yet Peterson is not a psychoanalyst, remember. He does not spend hours having the dreamer free-associate before he can decode the intricate symbolism of the dream. He simply *intuits* the meaning—as he intuits physical ills, life situations, and, on occasion, future events.

Returning to the matter of sexual symbolism in dreams, a sitter asked Peterson, "What are the spiritual implications of masturbation and homosexuality of males or females in dreams?"

Peterson replied: "Masturbation in the dream shows self satisfying self. Homosexuality would show what is evident in every soul, that it is both male and female. Often, dreams of what thou wouldst term homosexuality are only the touching of the soul-mind and its echoes of the *soul's* bisexuality. Sometimes such dreams can relate to homosexuality in the physical sense, but only sometimes. It depends upon the individual . . ."

A middle-aged man, discontented with his life, asked Peterson the meaning of the following dream: "I was in a large hardware store and it had lots of different kinds of materials in it. And the phone rang and I picked it up—which would be an unusual thing to do, but I did it—and a voice said: 'The big trailer has been given to you.'

"And I seemed to understand what that meant. Then my brother came along and said, 'What are you going to do with that big trailer?' And I said, 'I think I'll hunt up a man that needs the services of that trailer and hook his truck onto it and use it in his service.'"

Peterson interpreted the dream thus:

"What thou dost term the hardware store is thy consciousness, see? And what does the hardware contain? All the tools that thou needest to build what thou desirest to build—a more happy and contented life.

"The phone call is a message from thy soul-mind to thy consciousness. What thou hast been offered is a new way of life, is it not? The mobile home is a transition that is taking place in thy life, is it not?

"The answer thou gavest to thy brother's question—that thou wouldst hook thy trailer to the back of someone else's truck—indicates the manner in which thou has been accustomed to travel through life: being pulled by someone else.

"But there was more to the dream that thou didst not recall. For the truck was low on fuel and this was of concern to thee.

"However, where, in truth, dost thou receive thy fuel, thine energies? Dost thou not receive them from the creative forces themselves; from God, who is both passive and benevolent?

"As we see it, this dream would be helpful to thee in understanding thyself.

"Work with what thou hast at hand, for thou hast everything necessary to build a better life if thou wouldst but look for it and use it. This would apply to thy home, thy business, thy mind, thy soul.

"Do not depend on any other man to pull thee through life. Depend upon the God-force within thyself. For thou art part of God, as are all men, see? And if God be for thee, what truly can stand against thee?"

A young man reported to Ross Peterson the following colorful, somewhat grisly, and certainly paradoxical dream.

"In the city in Germany where I grew up I was sent to jail for a petty crime. I was let out on parole and went home reluctantly to tell my mother. Instead of understanding, she took a knife and cut both my feet off. In a rage, I killed her then with a knife and felt very satisfied over it.

"The dream ended by my being pursued by the police. Finally I was shot in the head and I was very satisfied about it."

Peterson's interpretation:

"The jail in which thou feelest imprisoned is thine own physical body. Compared to the dimension in which thou existed before entering the physical body, life in the body can be seen as an entrapment, an imprisonment. And the cause of the imprisonment? Thou didst indeed break the law—God's perfect law of sowing and reaping. That is the purpose of incarnation: to work out karmic problems and obligations.

"Now, there are times when the soul feels discouragement and seeks release, parole, from the body. But this only happens when the soul has temporarily lost sight of the reason for being in the body—to perfectly fulfill the law and return at last to the Godhead.

"Now, this losing sight of the purpose of life is what it means to have thy feet cut off. For without this knowledge of the purpose of life thy spiritual progress will be hampered. It would be as though thou tried to walk with no feet.

"Thy rage and taking of the knife to slay thy mother means the desire in thee to kill that part of thy self which blocks thy spiritual progress.

"Being pursued by the police refers to the law, God's law, the eternal law. There are no injustices in thy world. All is the result of sowing and reaping.

"Thy being shot indicates again thy desire to kill within thy consciousness that which is detrimental to thy spiritual progress. And this is why thou felt satisfied. Continue thy growth in spiritual understanding and thou wilt feel even more satisfied.

Peterson said that besides the basic spiritual meaning of this dream, there were secondary meanings.

"Thus," he added, "the knife in the dream can also be seen as pertaining to thy attitude toward the sharing of thy physical body through the manifestation of love with the opposite sex. Thy inability to share thy physical love causes the rage you feel in the dream. And thy subconscious mind is telling thee to seek ways of killing the attitudes within thyself which prevent the physical sharing of love. Look for an overattachment to the mother in thy childhood and youth."

A young married woman who was deeply into spiritual and psychic development and felt her failings acutely reported the following dream:

"I went to visit a home for deranged women, was shown around by the headmistress, who told me that they kept twenty to twenty-five women in the home. They were mildly disturbed and paraded around in various costumes.

"When it was time for me to go I couldn't find my purse; one of the women seemed to have hidden it. I looked in different rooms, all of them shabby.

"Later I found myself on a winding road, somewhat uphill. There were the ordinary road signs. While observing these I wondered why they had not also put up warning signs because there were floods throughout the countryside.

"My intention was to reach a bridge, which was only partly flooded, but before I could the road at its highest point came to an abrupt end and the car and I plunged down . . . into death.

"There was no panic on my part. It all seemed all right. The area on my side was green . . ."

Ross Peterson interpreted this as a very hopeful dream of spiritual progress.

"This dream reflects the question thou hast often asked thyself: Why am I? Why do I not do these things I know I ought to do?

"The house of deranged women shows the poor foundation, in this life and in some of thy previous lives, that thou hast laid for spiritual development. For the house represents thy consciousness, see?

"Searching for thy lost purse is looking for thy fortune, for the God within. And again, the dream comes now for this is a point in time when thou hast seriously set about seeking Him Who is to be found within.

"The winding road in the dream indicates thy tendency to vacillate from one extreme to another.

"The bridge would be crossing over—not the point that thou wouldst consider death but the point at which thou, as a soul, entered the flesh in this incarnation. For see, to be born could be construed as to die; and to die could be construed as to be born.

"At the point of crossover, the green area is showing thee that thou hast begun to harvest, that spiritual growth is being attained, that karmic rewards are due thee. See?"

In many of Peterson's interpretations is the implication that the dream is multi-layered, deriving some layers of meaning from this life, some from previous earth lives; some from the spiritual realm, and others from the physical side of life. In fact, the Peterson readings portray a dream as a veritable universe of meaning.

"Those things which are records of this life and past lives, recorded upon the skein of time and space, can be understood through learning the language of the soul, which is the dream.

"Work with what thou hast in hand; work with what thou hast now; carefully vow to meet thyself; improve thyself; and thou wilt naturally reap the harvest of the seeds thou hast sown. The study and the meaning of dreams should be the most important aspect of study in any man's language for it is the language of thyself; it is the language of thee and thy relationship to the universe; to the Godhead. See?"

According to the readings, the unconscious mind of each of us is omniscient about what is going on within our own bodies at any given time. The unconscious unfailingly monitors every physical process, every bodily change, however subtle, whether for good or ill.

An example of a medical self-diagnostic dream comes from Ross Peterson himself.

"Early in 1976, my dream, night after night, was this: I was walking down a stream and I would come to an elbow in the stream, or a bend in the stream, but it was all clogged up with brush, debris and rubbish. And I was fighting like the devil—with a rake one time and a hoe another time—to clear this debris out of this elbow of the creek because the water was backing up behind it and was going to flood things and make a hell of a mess.

"Now, at the same time that I was having this dream, night after night, the readings were urging me to have stomach surgery. Finally, they *ordered* me to have it, or else!

"Well, the surgeon who operated on me said that the reason I had been having so much of a problem—pain and inability to keep down food—was that in the lower pyloric region and the duodenum portion of my stomach there was a mass of scar tissue and it was causing an obstruction that the food couldn't pass.

"That's what I believe my recurrent dream was all about. Because invariably a person will dream of what they are concerned about *at that time*. And I was sure as hell concerned about my health at that particular time. So this is what my dreams reflected."

In trance, Peterson's *alter ego* confirms this maxim: What is concerning you is what your dreams are likely to be about.

If you are concerned about finances or material needs, your dreams will be about finances and material needs. If you are concerned about sex, your dreams will be about sex. If you are concerned about spiritual growth, your dreams will be about spiritual growth.

An important clue, then, to finding the key to your dream is to search your mind for an answer to the question: What, at this time in my life, am I most deeply concerned about? The answer to that question, says Ross Peterson, will indicate how your dream should be interpreted; on what level and in what terms.

More about dreams, how to remember yours, and the self-interpretation of them for spiritual growth is included in Chapter 14, "How to Become Your Own Seer."

Chapter Ten

READINGS ABOUT GOD
AND AN AFTERLIFE

Any theology is by its nature inaccessible to proof.

Strictly speaking, *proof* is possible only in mathematics and logic. In all other areas of thought, particularly where questions of value are paramount, the best we can attain are levels of probability.

The truth or falsity of any theology is a matter for individual judgment. The source of the theology should be considered; its reasonableness; and the emotive or intuitive response it evokes in the individual (which is usually what is meant by "faith").

The theology of the Ross Peterson readings—the concept of God, the soul, prayer and man's *post mortem* des-

tiny—is similar to what is found in the Edgar Cayce readings. Not being a deep student of the latter, I'm incapable
of judging precisely where the Peterson and Cayce readings converge and diverge theologically.

Some might argue that since Ross Peterson has already
demonstrated his genuine seership in areas where its accuracy *can* be verified—in medical clairvoyance, psychological profiles and predictions—its validity in theological
matters should simply be taken for granted.

However, this seems to me to be a dubious proposition.

Every experienced psychical researcher knows how the
paranormal perceptions of clairvoyants are colored, often
to a profound extent, by their religious beliefs, cultural
background and other influences. Thus Catholic mystics
see Christ in their visions; Hindu mystics see the Lord
Krishna; and spiritualist mediums see the spirits of the
departed.

These experiences may all be valid, in the sense that
they represent a contact with a genuine reality but obviously many of the *details* are influenced by what the individual expects to experience.

In Ross Peterson's case it is clear how derivative of
Cayce's his philosophy is. It may well be that Cayce was
in touch with Ultimate Truth and Peterson is simply tapping the same Source. However, it may also be that Peterson's ideas were unconsciously influenced to a marked degree by Cayce's.

It should be said here that Peterson strongly denies any
conscious borrowing from Cayce. In many instances he
has told me he was unaware that his readings corrobo-
rated what Cayce said on this or that matter.

Also, Peterson has been asked exotic, even bizarre questions which I doubt Cayce was ever asked, and his answers were prompt and delivered with the same familiar
assurance which pervades all the readings. One sitter, for
example, asked: "What were the secrets that were known

by the master violin makers of Italy which enabled them to make a superior varnish that cannot be duplicated at present?" Another sitter asked: "Can you give me an organic and effective control for the beetle which affects vine types of garden vegetables by damaging the stem at the base of the spine? Such vegetables as the cucumber, squash, pumpkin and watermelon."

Both these men got eloquent and detailed answers to their distinctly off-the-beaten-track queries.

At any rate, the theological concepts of the Ross Peterson readings are to be judged by you, the reader, in the light of your own experience.

What is the claimed Source of the Peterson theology?

This question was asked point-blank by a sitter: "Whom is it I am now talking to?"

The reply: "It is the higher self of this entity Peterson, in contact with those things which are recorded upon the skein of time and space. This mind goes to levels where it is directed, seeking out the information desired by the questioner. This is not a case of some other entity taking over this body but of the higher element of this entity seeking those levels where truth may be found, see?"

In another sitting the question was asked: "Can you give us the number of levels that exist from which this type of channel [Peterson] can obtain information?"

"For the finite mind," the entranced Peterson responded, "it would be best to think of the number as twelve. Understand that the level that ye are consistently in during the waking state is deemed to be one. When the mind is quieted, it would be as two. During natural sleep, ye would be at the third level, and occasionally touch the fourth.

"But as each soul becomes more willing to seek out the Godhead itself, it can reach higher and higher dimensions.

"Reaching the twelfth dimension would mean returning to the Godhead—so knowing the eternal law, so living the law, that ye *become* the law, as in expressing the Christ love. The Christ love has been demonstrated by many throughout the ages. There were some who lived in the six hundredth year before the coming of the Master, Jesus, in India and Asia, who attained Christ consciousness, as the Master did. Ye can attain the same also. It is the birthright of each soul.

"The other levels, identifying them by number, represent higher spheres which the entity reaches through perseverance, laying aside the small 'I am' and ever seeking the larger 'I AM,' which is the Godhead.

"This one through whom communication is now coming [Ross Peterson] has subjugated the consciousness so that it attains the sixth level easily, consistently works into the seventh, occasionally touches the eighth and has on two occasions touched the ninth, see?"

The same sitter then asked: "What was the highest level reached by Edgar Cayce?"

The reply: "He worked consistently on the seventh level, into the eighth, many times into the ninth and touched the tenth on numerous occasions."

Here, Peterson accords his mentor a slight seniority in the hierarchy of spiritual communication.

This, anyway, is what the readings themselves claim is their Source: higher levels of consciousness approaching, but not reaching, the Godhead itself.

What is the nature of God?

The readings convey what is technically called a pantheistic ("God is everything") and, more particularly, a pan*en*theistic ("God is every soul") concept of the Divine Being.

Some relevant excerpts from the readings:

"It is difficult for any finite human mind to grasp the infinitude, the unlimitedness of the God Force. If ye were to travel with 10,000 times the speed of light in any direction ye would never reach the limits of God, for there are none. . . .

"If ye would stand and look at the farthest star, know that God is there. And if ye were on that star and looked to the farthest star, know that God is there. . . .

"Gravity and all other forces in the universe and universes are God manifested in different forms. For all force is ultimately one Force, ye see, and that Force is God."

The readings, speaking of God as a "Force," suggest that the Cosmic Mind is not personal, at least in the sense in which most people use that term. Certainly God is not anthropomorphic, subject to human whims and vagaries like the Jehovah of the Old Testament. Yet nor is God merely an impersonal energy like electricity (though electricity is an emanation of His power). The readings stress that "God is Love," and love cannot be impersonal. Electricity never loved anybody.

Perhaps it is more accurate to say that God is impersonal not in the sense of being less than personal (like a blind energy) but *more* than personal, in that God as Love transcends the distinctions, discriminations and other attributes of personality which characterize human love even at its highest. The difference is that man loves, whereas God *is* Love.

The Godhead, in the Peterson readings, is *supra*personal.

How did individual souls or spirits come to exist? If the Godhead was and is All, whence came the separation into billions of separate centers of consciousness, occupying human bodies, which we call souls or minds?

The Peterson readings portray a cosmic drama in which God *chose* to individuate Himself. He divided Himself into separate entities whose purpose it was to pass through this world of time and space to learn lessons which even God could learn in no other way. In some in-

scrutable sense, God will be fuller, richer, greater for having individuated himself in billions of human forms.

The destiny of each soul is often repeated in the Peterson readings: "To return to thy Source."

When the complete return of mankind to God is accomplished; when all individuation is over and every soul
has merged once more into the Godhead—then, in some
incommunicable way, the Infinite will be more infinite;
the Perfect, more perfect; the One, even more one.

But before such a cosmic consummation can be
fulfilled, say the readings, "each soul must recognize that
it comes from God, that it is of God, that it is part of God,
and that the original separation was by choice. And the
purpose of the series of earthly lives is to return to the
beginning—union with the Godhead."

The readings teach that man's separation from God,
though real, is not Real with a capital R. Each of us is
linked to each other and to God still in the most intimate
way possible.

"Nothing is separate from God except thy thinking
processes," a reading said, "yet even they are related. It is
the self-imposed finitude of the human mind which brings
unhappiness or sorrow. For God is Infinite, God is Love,
Love is Law, Law is God, see? Ye are apart and separate,
but yet ye are part of the Whole. See?

Our link to God is through our "soul-mind," our deeper
mind, the levels that are reached in meditation.

"This soul-mind is thy direct link to those creative
forces which are of God and are God."

The challenge facing each human being is to come to
an inner realization of his oneness with God. This is
achieved by perfectly fulfilling the Law. And then comes
absorption back into the Godhead, "as the dewdrop
merges into the silver sea."

The reason for reincarnation—a series of earthly lifetimes for each soul—is that it takes time to acquire the

needed lessons, to perfectly fulfill the Law. Man returns to earth as often as necessary until he learns his spiritual lessons that must be learned.

The principle of moral cause and effect to which each and every human soul is subject is called the Law of Karma.

"We had best explain that which ye term karma," a reading said. "Ye must understand that karma is of self. All experiences, all alliances with others, should be regarded as an opportunity for the self to meet its own shortcomings. Ye meet yourself by reaping what ye have sown in previous lives. That which ye failed at in the past, ye have an opportunity to succeed at in the present. And the karma ye sow in this life shall be reaped, for gain or loss, in the next life."

But the wheel of rebirth does not revolve endlessly. It stops for the individual soul when that soul achieves the level of spiritual understanding and growth called the "Christ consciousness," as Jesus did.

The readings differ from orthodox Christianity (though they claim to have rediscovered and restated pure, uncorrupted Christianity) in drawing a sharp distinction between Jesus and the Christ.

A reading given for a clergyman expressed it thus: "It would be very helpful to thee if thou wouldst approach the question of Christ and Jesus from this concept.

"Thou speakest often of Christ. Thou shouldst understand as we believe thou dost, that Christ is a consciousness. Jesus was the man who was referred to as the Christ. However, this is a consciousness which is potentially obtainable by all if they are diligent in applying the truths they have.

"Even Jesus did not attain the Christ consciousness in one experience, for it took him, even he, thirty earth lifetimes to achieve Christhood. He did it by overcoming all temptations. He achieved the return to the Father from Whom he came."

In another reading, the entranced Peterson said: "Christ must be defined as a consciousness. Christ is of the mind. Christ and Love could be the same word. It was Jesus the man in one age; Christ in *all* ages. For Jesus the man did evolve to become the Christ. And as such became a co-creator with the God Force, but with *knowledge*, ye see. For all souls are creators or co-creators with God, but most are co-creators without knowledge. This is because thoughts are things, as real as anything ye know. And all souls think, and in thinking ye create!

"Those who begin to *understand* the law which is Love eventually *become* the law which is Love. When this has been reached, they have attained the Christ consciousness, as Jesus did."

One sitter asked: "By our calendar, what was the actual birthdate of Jesus?"

The reply: "By thy calendar . . . look for it on what ye would term the first day of spring. This would be the twentieth or twenty-first of March. At the witching hour, see?"

"And the year?" the sitter asked.

"As ye record time, 7 B.C."

"Did Jesus really rise from the tomb and ascend into heaven?"

"Yes, he did so, and took the body with him, as all can do if they follow the path that he has laid down."

"And what is heaven?"

"Heaven is a state of consciousness. Ye need not shed the physical body to experience heaven. For heaven is thine now, as hell is thine now. It depends upon what ye do with choice, the greatest power ye have, thy will."

The Law was succinctly expressed in a reading in ten pregnant words: "Whatever thou doest to another person, thou doest to thyself."

The Peterson readings caution that achieving the Christ consciousness is no easy task and warn against undue zeal or fanaticism in the quest.

Attaining any spiritual level cannot be forced. Some individuals, according to the readings, can be overeager. They try to burst into Christhood in one mighty leap. This is dangerous.

"Gradually grow in spirituality," a reading counseled. "Gradually enter higher spheres. Do so carefully. Do so patiently. For if ye do not, it would be the same as giving a cup of salt to an infant—it would kill him. Yet a little salt is necessary. See?

"Even on occasions when this entity [Peterson] has touched the ninth level of consciousness, the highest he has achieved, there was a resultant great confusion in his mind and if he had stayed there too long he would have awakened feeling demented.

"Thou must be patient in thine endeavor to reach ever upward so that thou canst return to that from whence thou comest."

A reading warned one woman that her overzealousness in trying to achieve instant Christhood was "carrying thee to extremes." She was developing a martyr complex, allowing others to trample on her, exploit her and transgress against her—not only without any protest but with her blessing.

To try to demonstrate "Christ love" prematurely, said Peterson, is to invite ruin into our practical lives and affairs. Only a Christ can handle the dynamite which Christ love is, said the reading.

"There can be dangerous excesses in trying to attain the Christ love. Thou cannot attain it in deed until thou hast truly attained it in consciousness. And consider what that would mean.

"One who is truly as loving as Christ would let even the most heinous of murderers continue to commit yet another act and would love him as much as he would love those who are seemingly graceful and spiritual in form and manner. For there is absolutely no bias, no prejudice, no distinction in Christ love. For the true Christ loves all, anything of any dimension. See?

"Only Christ love can truly say on the cross: 'Father, forgive them for they know not what they do.'"

The readings define sin as simply failing to will for others what we will for ourselves. Such conventional virtues as abstinence from alcohol or tobacco are not commended, though moderation is.

"Eight to ten cigarettes a day never hurt anyone," was the reply to one questioner who asked about the morality of smoking. Another reading, replying to whether the use of alcohol was sinful, said: "No, only in excess. Wine, red wine, can be a healthful food and tranquilizer for the body. But only the red wine. And only in moderation. A few ounces a day, with meals or before retiring."

The readings deny the existence of the traditional devil.

"Selfishness to the nth degree is the devil. But the devil as an incarnate or personal being does not exist. This concept is simply a device which has been used to control men's minds through fear."

What is prayer?

"Prayer," say the readings, "is thought. What thy thoughts dwell upon, that is thy prayer. So be careful. That for which thou prayest may indeed come to thee.

"No prayers that are held in the heart are ever denied. The *fear* which thou holdest in thy mind will also be answered, for that is prayer also, is it not?"

In other words, prayer is not something you say but a state of mind or being. Thus, to "pray without ceasing," as the Bible enjoins, means to maintain constantly a correct state of mind.

What happens to the soul after death in the intermission between earthly lifetimes? This question was asked by a woman physician.

The answer, in substance, was that the soul ascends to the level which it is suited to and distills from the memories of the lifetime just lived the lessons to be learned—the failures and the successes. Then, after a period of reflection which may vary from a few days or weeks to many years, the soul decides to plunge again into this world of time and space to continue the pilgrimage back to the Father's House.

"As ye pass through God's other door, which ye call death, ye take with ye that which ye have been," the reading said.

"Some spend a few days, as few as eight, in a state of limbo, confusion, purgatory, as the Catholic would call it, when there is a lack of awareness that the death of the physical body has occurred.

"Some, who died in gross spiritual ignorance, might spend as long as eight hundred years, in terms of earth time, in this particular level. This is because everything they love is of the earth and they have no desire to leave it.

"But eventually all—except those who have elected to cast themselves into darkness—will find that they are surrounded by companions who are only too willing to help them as they continue to evolve.

"The soul leaves the record of what it has been on earth behind it. This is registered upon the skein of time and space and it appears as a shell, so to speak, of the total entity, for the soul has gone on to other spheres.

"Those who elect to re-enter this earth sphere take on that shell once more. All that they have been is again a portion of the whole, and they carry this with them when they reassume a physical body."

The quintessence of the philosophy of the Ross Peterson readings is summed up in a passage which I think is beautifully expressed.

"A life that is lived and has not learned to love is a life that is wasted. It has gained not a whit.

"Learn to love thy God with all thy heart, thy mind, thy body and thy soul. Learn to love thyself, for thou art God and of God. Learn to love thy brother as thyself, for he is but an extension of thyself.

"Learn to love where thou art, whom thou art with and that which thou art doing.

"For love is the fulfilling of the law."

Chapter Eleven

WHAT THE READINGS TEACH ABOUT MARRIAGE, DIVORCE, ABORTION, AND SEX AND SAINTHOOD

Marriages—true marriages—*are* made in heaven. Literally, not metaphorically.

A dead marriage may be resurrected, but if it proves to be beyond resurrection there is no sin in divorce.

Abortion is at most a misdemeanor and emphatically not a serious sin.

And sexual abstinence, even for married couples, is usually an important and natural step on the road to saintliness.

These are some of the provocative, often surprising, observations from the Ross Peterson readings on that most important of human relationships, marriage. In some instances—as in their rather *laissez-faire* attitude toward abortion, viewing it as a venial transgression, if a transgression at all—the Peterson readings are no doubt highly controversial.

But each of the positions stated is logical within the structure of the philosophy of the readings, when one examines the reasoning behind it.

Take what the readings say about the nature, essence and dissolubility versus indissolubility, of marriage.

To begin with, the readings are pro-marriage, in contrast to the surrogates for marriage which are gaining increasing popularity in our permissive society.

"Is traditional marriage a better arrangement than simple cohabitation or a trial marriage?" asked a young male college student.

"Marriage always was and always will be the better way," replied the entranced Peterson, "for without it there is no commitment. It is not that living together is a sin, if there is love—for it is not. Rather, it is a matter of which is the better form for commitment to take. For without the concept of a legal commitment held in the mind, can there really be commitment? Without the legal ties, cannot any commitment be dissolved more readily, more easily? Therefore, is not the commitment in legal marriage stronger, deeper, because it can less easily be broken?

"That which ye call traditional marriage is closer to God's plan, though it is not the words said over ye that are vital so much as the true commitment of the heart to each other. However, most people are so permeated with the doctrine that unless there is the legal tie there is no real commitment, it is doubtful whether they are capable of truly feeling a commitment without that legal bond.

"This is true for thee who puts this question. Ask thyself: Dost thou truly feel married in thy present circumstances or art thou merely sharing the bed?"

For most people, say the Peterson readings, marriage is the best way. There are a few people who can lead a single life and be very contented but they are rare individuals. Most who remain single, say the readings, are missing opportunities for further soul development.

Marriage affords the greatest opportunities for spiritual advancement. Of course, "marriage" here can be interpreted, for those of homosexual persuasion, as a lasting relationship between two people based on mutual love. The essence of marriage is not physical anyway, say the readings, but a merging of minds, hearts, personalities and, in rare cases, souls.

"Marriage gives rich opportunities for spiritual growth," said a reading (possibly not without a trace of irony, "because it is the most trying situation that can be experienced in the flesh.

"By the same token, however, it can be the most rewarding."

The concept of marriages being made in heaven is something which the readings take literally in terms of a sort of celestial biochemistry.

"A physicist might explain the attraction which exists in a true marriage in this fashion," said the readings.

"Each body has a certain element of magnetic power, operating either on the positive or the negative side. It is like the two poles of a magnet.

"If each human being had no wayward desires but was exactly as God intended him or her to be, they would be attracted only to the one who perfectly complemented them. Alas, this is often not the case. The perfect attraction of God's magnetism is distorted by human willfulness and lust and selfishness, and so imperfect marriages often result.

"But from the imperfection great spiritual growth may come."

The greatest sin in marriage, according to the Peterson

readings, is the desire of one partner to dominate the other and in so doing to rob him or her of their individuality.

"Regard marriage as an agreement to share the rest of your lives together. But encourage each other to be as independent as possible, yet so loving and compassionate that ye can depend upon each other in a time of storm or crisis."

What about divorce?

One of the worst possible sins, say the readings, is to stay in a marriage where love has died. This is a "mental divorce" without the courage or responsibility of taking the step of full dissolution of the marriage. And the readings warn that this kind of situation is soul-destroying.

"I was astounded to hear one reading say that killing somebody, in some circumstances, may not be half so sinful as two people agreeing to continue living together for appearances' sake when love has gone," said Ross Peterson.

This is not to say that the readings sanction easy divorce. They do not, although they do teach that in some cases divorce is not a sin, because it is inevitable.

If, for example, one spouse decides to grow spiritually in the marriage, to become more compassionate, more loving, more giving and forgiving, less judgmental, hateful, greedy and lustful, while the other partner refuses to change—then it is inevitable that eventually there will be a divorce. But before divorce is the spiritually right thing to do, the readings lay down a rather stringent proviso.

"What should be done by the partner who is sincere in seeking to follow God's plan is to do what the Master and the other masters always have done—which is to set an example.

"Take a pencil and write down everything that a perfect husband or wife would do. Then practice these things for at least three cycles of the moon.

"After the three moon cycles, look into the mirror, so thou canst see into thine own eyes, and ask thyself, 'Have I truly done my best?' Search thy heart before answering this question.

"If thou dost feel truly that the answer is yes, and thy married lot has *not* improved, then seek a divorce. But if thy marriage has improved, and it almost certainly will as the other partner responds to thine example, then continue setting an example for another three cycles of the moon.

"In this way, a dead marriage can be regenerated. It is the old, familiar law—ye receive only what ye give."

However, if, after an honest attempt to go the second and the third mile in reactivating love within the marriage, the other partner fails to respond, then divorce is justified.

Abortion, as the readings see it, is a minor sin, if indeed it be a sin. The key to this view is what the readings say about the process of "ensoulment" and the nature of the embryo before ensoulment occurs.

In reply to a sitter who admitted she was contemplating an abortion and asked for guidance, a reading said: "We will help thee to understand what is involved and then the choice is thine to make.

"From conception, there is within the embryo a form of consciousness—what ye would term the subconscious, see? This is only a small part of the total entity and is like a mechanical recording device that functions until the infant is delivered. This recording device is not the soul. And the embryo is not a human being, in the true sense, until the soul enters this vegetative being in the womb.

"While the physical vehicle is being created within the womb there may be from one to 201 souls hovering around the body of the mother. The time of ensoulment, when the embryo or fetus becomes a living soul, a true human being, varies greatly.

"The soul generally enters the body within the day after the child is delivered from the womb. But sometimes it does not enter until two or three days after the child is delivered.

"Sometimes a soul will enter the body and find it not to its liking and another will enter, see?

"If ye were to take the life of the embryo or fetus before the soul has entered its body, what would ye have taken? Merely the physical life, no different from the life of a rabbit.

"And what have ye denied? There is only a simple denial of the opportunity for a soul to enter that body at that point in time. But the soul is eternal and has plenty of time.

"Would ye feel guilty for destroying a mere recording device? For this is fundamentally what the embryo or fetus is until the soul, with its memories, its experiences, its awareness, enters into that physical form.

"We see no crime in expelling the embryo or fetus from the body, other than that the body of the mother is temporarily disrupted and illness might follow. But what ye term sin? We see none.

"It is not for us to say what is right or wrong in any individual case. This is the choice of the parents concerned, and chiefly the mother. We do say that it is wrong for anyone else to judge another, whatever her choice may be in this matter."

Ross Peterson admits that in his conscious state he was surprised and somewhat discomposed when he first heard a reading discuss abortion and its relation to the process of ensoulment. It ran contrary to his preconceptions about the embryo or fetus as fully human.

"The readings say that sometimes two or three souls

will try a body on for size, so to speak, before permanent ensoulment occurs," Peterson said.

"I wondered about cases where ensoulment might take place as early as the seventh month of pregnancy and then an abortion was done. Wouldn't this be the destruction of a human being? But the readings assure us that the soul is aware of the possibility that an abortion might occur and will not inhabit that body.

"So what is extinguished when an embryo is aborted is simply the activating principle of life in the lowest sense—the same activating principle that a cow has, or a rabbit, or any other animal. These do not have souls. They have instinct but not intelligence. And the difference is that instinct is something genetically programmed while intelligence involves the ability to gather new facts or relearn old facts that have been forgotten, and the faculty of making moral choices.

"Now, animals, in this sense, do not have intelligence and nor does the embryo. And the reason is that neither is a living soul. The soul is the seat of intelligence."

What about celibacy?

The readings teach that this is very much a matter of the individual case. To attempt to live a celibate life in order to attain a "higher" level of consciousness is a great mistake for many people. On the other hand, there are those, say the readings, who naturally grow into celibacy. Indeed, it seems to be an invariable signpost on the road to saintliness or the development of the Christ consciousness.

Consider some excerpts from the readings.

A young male college student asked: "Is chastity beneficial to the spiritual self?"

"Occasionally it is," the reading replied. "But thou wilt find that if the carnal mind has not been satisfied chastity will be more detrimental than beneficial. For even if thou dost deny thyself physical congress with the opposite sex, is not thy mind filled with lustful thoughts?

"Chastity is self-deceit if the mind entertains lustful thoughts. We say *entertains* them, which implies providing hospitality. For the lustful thought is real—as real as the deed.

"But if the mind holds not lustful thoughts and chastity is practiced, then there is the raising of those forces within the body which enable one to gain inspiration from the very Fountainhead, what thou wouldst term universal consciousness. See?

"Until the mind is filled with joy, until the mind is filled with love, it is natural to have carnal thoughts and desires, and to satisfy these is not sinful if love is present. Yet there is a higher way. . . ."

The higher way, the readings say, is a celibacy or sexual abstinence which grows naturally out of a profound desire.

"I have come to see," said Ross Peterson, "that some people can live in a state of sexual abstinence and be perfectly contented with it. And if they're married their mate will be contented with it too. I don't think anybody should impose abstinence on him or herself but just let it happen, if it's going to, as a natural feeling.

"Anybody who is moving toward sainthood, whether they realize it consciously or not, will reach the stage of natural celibacy or sexual abstinence.

"The reasoning here, from the readings, is that sexual power and spiritual power are the very same power. And when a person becomes centered upon developing the God within him then all the power is used in that effort and sexual expression is forgotten.

"Commonly, this is called sublimation of sex. And that's literally true. In this sort of sexual abstinence the sex drive is truly sublimated—*made sublime.* It's subjugated but not forcibly. Sex simply becomes subject to the greater drive to achieve Christ consciousness.

"So the psychiatrist Carl Jung was right when he said that the lust for God is stronger than the lust for sex. Freud was wrong. Sex is important and for most people necessary, but it's not the *raison d'être* of life. Reunion with the Godhead is the greatest passion of which man is capable."

Thus say the Peterson readings.

Chapter Twelve

THE SHAPE OF THINGS THAT WERE

Atlantis. Mu. Lemuria.

Are these alleged lost civilizations fact or fiction?

The Ross Peterson readings, like Edgar Cayce's, declare that these legendary worlds once existed upon the earth and that evidence of them is being uncovered and will continue to be uncovered.

According to the Peterson readings, Atlantis began 78,000 years before the birth of Christ. This pushes the dawn of civilization on earth back much further than orthodox archaeology or history allow. Yet the readings contend that not only was Atlantis truly civilized but eventually it was as high, or higher, technologically and culturally, than our own civilization.

"Through the development of this particular portion of the world over thousands and thousands of years," say the readings, "it evolved from the simplest form of gathering fruits and vegetables to sustain the body to actually producing what was known as the very ether from the air itself to regenerate tissues."

The readings see human evolution as very much an oscillating process, swinging between the polarities of growth and decline.

"Atlantean culture grew a day at a time . . . a line at a time . . . a jot or a tittle at a time. Fire was discovered once again, for the ability to utilize it had been lost. But it had been lost many times before and discovered many times again."

From a predominantly agrarian, peaceable society Atlantis changed into a militaristic culture. Some 62,000 years B.C., say the readings, the warlike Atlanteans raided and plundered the lands of other peoples more primitive than themselves and brought back a multitude of slaves. "Atlantis became a slavery-based society. And this," say the readings, "is what ultimately proved to be its undoing.

"Study the history of other nations known to ye," advise the readings, "and ye will find that as it was done then, so it was done in the Atlantean land.

"There were surges. There was knowledge and then this was lost. And then there were surges again when man did seek through avenues of expression, through mathematics, through music, through poetry, through all aspects of learning, to return from whence he came.

"But it would always be three steps forward and two back; then three steps forward and two back.

"For when man begins to prosper, as he did in the

Atlantean experience, he forgets the Godhead. He remembers God only when there is difficulty and suffering. As man's vanity and ego grow, the soul portion, his link to God, is forgotten as it was then in Atlantis."

According to the readings, the cyclic spiral of Atlantean civilization—rising and falling, only to rise again—followed a pattern of about 1,200 years of advance succeeded by 3,000 years of decline into a dark age. Then, again, renewal and growth.

Atlantis ultimately occupied a land mass stretching from near the coast of modern Florida to Spain. Submarine upheavals and quakes eventually broke this land mass up into five giant islands. But this was not the end of Atlantis. The civilization withstood these natural cataclysms and continued to prosper. Indeed it flourished even more vigorously and reached transcendent heights before it finally, in effect, committed suicide. Its collapse was an act of self-destruction.

"Atlantis reached its peak about 32,000 years before the coming of the Master," said a reading.

"This was when there were secrets unlocked that are being rediscovered today—the secrets of harnessing the sun's energy, concentrating it, focusing it and storing it.

"These forms of capturing nature's energy were used to rejuvenate bodies, to activate the growth of plants, for the transporting of freight, goods and bodies through the air, in various vehicles. Look to the ways that ye use energy now, and know that they were followed then in the same fashion. But even more so, see?"

There were glittering cities the length and breadth of Atlantis. Yet in the same period "giant beasts" (as the Peterson readings call them) roamed the uncivilized portions of the world and from time to time made incursions into the boundaries of Atlantis.

"There were gatherings of people from many parts of

the lands in order to discover ways of best eradicating these creatures from the face of the earth as man is wont to do," say the readings.

It would seem (though the readings are not totally clear on the point) that what ultimately became the instrument of Atlantis' self-destruction was originally created to facilitate the eradication of the huge beasts. This was what the readings refer to as "certain crystals."

"There were three such crystals. They were called the giant crystals. But giant referred to their energy, not their actual size. Do not imagine that it takes huge size to create the terrible crystal. All three of the terrible crystals of Atlantis could be held in two hands. See?"

As has been intimated, the Atlantean civilization was rocked by several cataclysms before the final, man-made, one which plunged that glamorous civilization into the sea. The Peterson readings date these cataclysms and describe their nature and consequences.

"The first inundation, of natural origin, was approximately 32,000 years before the coming of the Master, when there was a breaking up of the solid Atlantean land mass into five islands by disruptions from the very bowels of the earth.

"The second inundation was approximately 28,000 years before the coming of the Master. And a final inundation struck approximately 12,000 years before the coming of the Master.

"This final inundation was not of natural origin. It was caused by men's inability to understand the power that was being gathered and harnessed and stored. And the rays of certain crystals which men were using as focusing points, or energy sources, were turned inward toward the very bowels of the earth and these activated forces there which caused stupendous earthquakes and tidal waves and the eventual collapse and sinking of those lands into the seas."

Peterson warns, in the readings, that history may be preparing to repeat itself. All those in important leadership positions in today's society, say the readings, are reincarnate Atlanteans. They are about to face the same sort of crisis which destroyed them once. Will they reenact their own destruction or, having learned the soul lessons needed, be able to avert it?

"Know ye," say the readings, "that there is danger again arising, in this very day. For the same power as of the crystal of Atlantis is now being developed and utilized. And eventually those which are known as the terrible crystals could again be produced, as they inevitably will be. See?

"What was lived in Atlantis is being lived now. Most of those now in the flesh who are bringing forth new scientific discoveries are the same souls who made these discoveries before. The new discoveries are but ancient discoveries which they are touching upon now as they did then."

Where did the refugees from Atlantis go before the ultimate convulsion?

The Peterson readings say that they fanned out in vast migrations to many different parts of the world.

"There was a large influx into what is called Egypt. There were large migrations that went to Spain, into the mountains of the Pyrenees. Even now there is a language spoken there that is almost pure Atlantean—that of the Basque tongue.

"A great many migrated to that portion of the world that is the isthmus between the North and South American continents, what is now Mexico, Central America.

"There were some Atlantean refugees who settled in

the Peruvian area and merged with the descendants of immigrants from Mu, which had been destroyed much earlier."

Mu, or Lemuria, according to the readings, was a glittering civilization which occupied an enormous land mass in the Pacific. It experienced a fate like that of Atlantis many, many centuries before.

"It was 50,700 years ago when the continent of Mu or Lemuria did perish," said a reading.

Many refugees from Mu, or Lemuria, made their way to what is now India and seeded there a culture of advanced philosophy and sophisticated arts and letters.

What evidences are there that Atlantis and Mu ever existed?

The Peterson readings declare that the discovery of underwater ruins off the island of Bimini in 1968 and 1969 is an important step toward eventually proving the historicity of Atlantis.

These ruins, which are said to cover an area of approximately eighty square miles between the Bahamian islands of Bimini and Andros, have been intensively investigated by Dr. Manson Valentine, honorary curator of the Miami Museum of Natural Science. Dr. Valentine, whose Ph.D. is from Yale and who has taught at several universities, is an expert in American origins. He has expressed his opinion that the underwater ruins in the Bahamas are a tangible remnant of the lost civilization of Atlantis.

The ruins are made up of a large templelike building, an obviously man-made wall which runs for fifty miles along the ocean floor, and gigantic circular shapes in very deep water which may be mammoth sports arenas or similar structures. Dr. Valentine described the underwater site to me as "a huge metropolitan complex."

These undersea structures are elements of Atlantis, say the Peterson readings.

"The square structure first discovered was a portion of the temple. And also discovered nearby is that which was a playing yard for certain games that the Atlanteans did use—that of driving a small stone through a stone ring that was mounted at each end of a long pit.

"There are further explorations taking place there even now."

The readings also speak of traces of the sunken continent of Mu lying on the bottom of the Pacific.

"There have been discoveries made," said a reading, "by those who have extended underwater the viewing apparatus that is electrical in nature. They have seen remnants of tall columns standing upright upon the ocean floor. These are not a natural formation but are manmade.

"If ye would look in the area of Peru, on the mountaintops, ye would find large stone tablets bearing the language of Mu. Buried in hidden archives in India, yet to be discovered, are the keys to deciphering the language of that ancient civilization."

As the Peterson readings describe it the sweep of human history is unimaginably vast, awesome, stretching back farther than the mind can grasp.

"If ye would go beyond Atlantis, beyond Mu, ye could touch civilizations and civilizations and still more civilizations. . . . They have existed for eons of time upon the earth, as they do now. And civilizations will continue. As one falls, another arises. This is man's way . . . his groping to learn to return to that from whence he has come. . . .

"But remember, man did not come from Atlantis or Mu or the civilizations before them. Man came from the

Godhead itself and unto the Godhead he must return. And return he shall, until every single soul has entered the Christ consciousness and the wheel of rebirth will stop, never to turn again. . . ."

Chapter Thirteen

THE SHAPE OF THINGS TO COME

What lies ahead for mankind?

In trance, Ross Peterson has traced a global scenario for the future highlighted by colossal geological changes, possible atomic war, economic collapse, climaxed by the metamorphosis of the Christian Church and "the second Coming of Christ."

Here are some of the specifics, as the readings have given them.

There is the possibility of nuclear war between 1984 and 1987. "It need not be," said a reading, "but in inspecting the laws of probability it is likely to be so. For that is man's way, see?"

Immense geological and topographical upheavals are forecast over the next thirty years.

"When ye look for the chaos beginning, look to Georgia and Carolina, see? There will be a sinking in this particular portion of the country.

"What ye call Manhattan must sink into the sea around the year 2006. The greater part of what ye call Los Angeles will plunge under water. The seas will then pour through an opening in the mountain chain and flood the San Joaquin Valley, where the major part of your country's vegetables are now grown. This, and part of Nevada, will become one huge inland sea. The greater part of the southern coast of California must expire.

"The greater portion of what is now Japan will plunge beneath the sea. Large portions of what ye term Europe will vanish as in the batting of an eye. Look for Spain, Portugal, portions of Italy to sink. Not in your lifetime, perhaps, but it will happen. . . .

"Ireland and the western part of England will experience massive inundations around the turn of the century . . . before 2030.

"There is a ring of fire—we call it this—which extends through Japan, upper Alaska, Washington, Oregon, California, around to the Borneo islands. Within this ring of fire great disruptions of the earth will occur. . . ."

The Peterson readings, continuing their apocalyptic vision, picture reversal of the direction of flow of the St. Lawrence River. Instead of emptying into the Atlantic, this great river will start dumping its water through Lake Michigan into the Mississippi and this will flood the delta region of the southern states.

"Louisiana, Mississippi will be a great inland sea," said a reading.

In 1989 or 1990 major earthquakes are foreseen in the northwest part of the United States or the southwest part of Canada.

Accompanying these tremendous natural cataclysms will be economic collapse. But the readings deny that these prognostications—worldwide geological upheavals and economic chaos—are necessarily grounds for pessimism. Not from the soul's view at any rate.

"Know ye," assure the readings, "that in any suffering, any chaos, any disruption, there is a blessing if ye would but sift it out. It would be like finding a precious diamond in a mountain of coal but it can be done. For if ye look for that diamond of truth amidst all earthly troubles ye find the portion that is God.

"It is only through disruption or chaos that the masses of men begin to turn to that which is within. That is when they beseech their God, 'O God, do help me!' And they return to the simple ways. They return to that which is the fulfilling of the purpose of life itself."

The vast changes forecast in the readings are said to presage a worldwide spiritual renaissance. . . .

"The next great awakening of Christianity will be in the land of the Bear, in Russia. Christianity will experience a rebirth there. But it will be a practical Christianity, that of applying the Godforce in everyday life. There will be a meeting of the scientific and the religious or philosophical mind.

"But it will be in Asia that the truly great spiritual awakening occurs. That which is the strongest part of Christianity, Catholicism, will spring up anew in the Asian countries. However, it will be modified to conform more closely to the true teachings of Jesus, the Master. For ye will find that the ancient Asian concept of reincarnation will be wedded, as it originally was, to the traditional teachings of Catholicism and from this marriage a new faith will emerge. It will lead to a thousand years of light and love demonstrated in the experience of man."

The Peterson readings predict sixteen more popes

after Paul VI, the current pontiff of the Roman Catholic Church.

"As *ye* know them, sixteen more," the reading said. "But when there are modifications they will continue on and on. For man must seek a representation of God in the flesh. That is why ye have the Pope. And man will always need that. Until all men awaken . . ."

Amidst the predicted physical chaos and economic confusion, the world will experience a climatic spiritual event in 1998 or 1999, promise the Peterson readings. This is what has traditionally been called "the second coming of Christ."

"But what is it that comes? Christ must be defined as a consciousness. The second coming of Christ is when masses and masses of men seek God first, God *first*. All other things second. And this will come, in the midst of earth's troubles. Men, amid the darkness, will see God's light in the sky."

Chapter Fourteen

HOW TO BECOME YOUR OWN SEER

Ross Peterson is utterly sincere in his contention that "anybody can learn to do what I do—if they are prepared to pay the price."

And the price is not money but effort, diligence, self-searching, a kind of psychological death and rebirth.

"I don't believe a person would have the motivation to stick to the necessary program of consciousness-expansion unless there has first been a spiritual awakening," Peterson said.

"There has to be an acceptance that everything we see is the end result of God—and we're a part of it and we're all interrelated. Which simply boils down to this: What we do to another, we do to ourselves. We come to accept this to the point that we really do have at least a touch of empathy for the other guy, the other person. Regardless of whether they're a native in the upper regions of the Amazon or whether they're part of a small ethnic group in Toronto, New York or Los Angeles.

"As you accept the spiritual aspects of life—that there is a force available to us (whether this force *is* God or is *of* God is a question I'm indifferent to; it doesn't make any difference to me any more) and that this force, working through our minds, can enable us to do anything we want in life; when you begin to accept that, then you begin to understand men like Jesus.

"They called him the Master. And he wasn't misnamed. He *was* a *Master*. He was a master of the mind. He understood fully God's law.

"But I think that anyone who firmly makes up his or her mind to work within the harmony of God's law can be another Jesus."

The unspoken addendum to Peterson's statement is: Though it may take many lifetimes to do it. However, a start, a very significant start on becoming another Jesus can be made by anybody, anywhere, anytime. And as individuals move forward in their spiritual growth, says Ross Peterson, they are bound to develop the same kind of psychic powers he has developed.

"The best way to develop your spiritual and psychic potential," he said, "is, ideally, to work with a teacher. And as in yoga, the best teacher is one who has traveled the path you wish to take.

"We have the example of Jesus, the greatest teacher ever known. Now, he didn't tell people to go out and find the burning bush themselves and receive the divine illumination. He said, 'I will teach you.' And he taught by showing or demonstrating.

"Now, that's what I want to do. My goal in life is not to

go on giving readings—I could never give enough in a lifetime to satisfy the demand. Rather, I want to teach others how to do what I do. To become their own psychic vehicles. Then they're no longer dependent upon me or any other person but themselves. That's the ideal."

However, Ross Peterson is perfectly aware that there are many sincere seekers after spiritual and psychic growth who, for any one of many valid reasons, *can't* spend the necessary time with a teacher (even if there are enough qualified teachers to go around). And these individuals need not despair.

"It's possible to do it all on your own. After all, *I* did. And now others can benefit from my experience. I'm going to set out here a detailed program for do-it-yourself psychic development which will enable anyone who sticks to it to reach the level of psychic functioning I've reached.

"The first step is to gain all the knowledge you possibly can about man's psychic nature. The libraries have an endless array of books on every subject in the psychic field. Go to the library and find all the books you can on the psychic. And especially on the art of meditation. Read them, so you can form your own opinion of what it's all about. Then begin to practice meditation on a daily basis.

"Please do not be excessive in it. In fact, no more than ten minutes, twice a day, should be spent in meditation in the early stages.

"Now be prepared to use some stick-to-itiveness. No one else can meditate for you. There's no such thing as meditation by proxy, any more than there is salvation by proxy. *You* must do it: Ten minutes a day, twice a day, but diligently, faithfully, every single day.

"The second path to becoming psychic safely without becoming psychotic—and you can follow this along with your meditation sessions—is dream interpretation.

"Now, if you say you don't dream, you're to be pitied.

If that is true, you're either psychotic or in the deep stages of drug addiction or alcoholism.

"What most people really mean when they say they don't dream is that they don't *remember* their dreams. Well, start remembering them. Here's how.

"Keep a dream diary. Begin by repeating an affirmation each night before you go to sleep. As you are relaxing yourself just prior to dropping off to sleep, simply declare to yourself, 'Tonight I will remember my dreams and as soon as a dream is completed, I will awaken briefly, record a key word or two, and then recall the whole of it in the morning.' Have a tape recorder by your bedside, or if you can't afford that, a pencil and a piece of paper.

"Now, you may go three or four days or even three or four weeks before you actually begin to remember the whole of your dreams. At first, you might just get dream fragments. But again, with perseverance, and practice, eventually you will become skilled at remembering almost all the dreams that you have during the night.

"As to how to interpret your dreams, that too will come with knowledge and practice. There is much excellent material available on dream interpretation. Don't limit yourself to one source. Read broadly to get a grasp of what dream symbolism is all about.

"Gather some Freud. Gather some Jung. Get some Edgar Cayce material. Get some books by such dreamologists as Calvin Hall and other contemporary psychologists. Soak yourself in these books. If you fill your mind with the bits of information you pick up from this book and from that book, your unconscious mind will record them, and later will bring them back to you as a meaningful message whenever you need them."

As you faithfully record your nocturnal dramas in your dream diary, said Ross Peterson, you will find them providing important clues to your spiritual and psychic progress.

"As an example, here's a dream that was quite profound that I had after I had begun to practice abstinence from alcohol and was deeply interested in the nature of God and the meaning of life. I was asking desperately for help, for understanding.

"In this dream I found myself on top of a mountain surrounded by a brick wall. The top of the mountain was very small—probably no more than fifty yards across. It was completely flat. And the wall was three or four feet high, beautifully constructed, and completely surrounding the top of the mountain.

"I walked over to the left and, looking down into the valley, I saw the ruins of a city smoking and smoldering, as after a fire.

"I walked over to the right, and as I walked to the right I noticed, coming over the horizon, a blinding white light. It was all-encompassing and dazzling to the point that I could not stand to look at it for fear of being blinded. So I dropped to my knees and hid behind the wall. But I felt the light showering upon me, almost like a brilliant satellite orbiting overhead, yet so blinding in its intensity that I knew I couldn't look at it.

"I worked with the dream and the interpretation I came up with—and you, too, will find the skill of deciphering your own dreams growing with study and practice—was as follows:

"I've learned that in my dreams, anything I see on the left-hand side is my material expression of life. Those smoldering ruins were the life I had just left. Now, what I see on the right-hand side in my dreams pertains to the spiritual aspect of my life. And it was a prognostication of what was to come. The light was coming but I was still afraid of it, so to speak. Light to me represents knowledge, energy, God-awareness. The light was coming and I could see it but I was such a spiritual babe I was still frightened by it.

"And the wall? It was the protective device that I had placed around myself—protecting myself with my personality. The top of the mountain showed the degree of my aspirations. I wanted to reach no less than the Godhead itself, or as close to heaven as I could get.

"Then, as my spiritual and psychic growth continued—and it is a growth, remember, not something that happens overnight—I had dreams that I was fishing. I soon learned that fishing and water have a spiritual connotation in my dreams, and these dreams reflected my development.

"When I first started dreaming about water and fish, I was fishing in muddy water and I was catching what you could call low forms of fish, like carp and bullheads. In one dream I caught a big, black whale that had a mouthful of wicked teeth. But the teeth fell out. Now, I had this dream shortly before I recognized that my excessive deceit and pathological lying were a no-no which had to be eliminated from my character at all costs, regardless of who was hurt. Which was me, first.

"I've learned that in my dreams, teeth falling out usually indicate deceit as a problem. Sometimes, of course, such a dream may be warning you that you actually have got bad teeth or a condition like pyorrhea. But when the dream has a spiritual meaning—and this is something you get a feel for with practice—losing teeth seems to pertain to deceit as the problem to be overcome. At least, in my dream symbolism.

"Fish to me represents spiritual food. A whale is not a fish, which indicated to me that I was eating false food. Also it was black, which suggested that I was looking predominantly on the dark side of things and still had a lot to learn.

"Then I went through a phase in my life when I was very aggressive. I wouldn't let anybody talk me out of anything. The fish that I caught in my dreams in this period were always pike or muskelunge, which are predators. The pike has a lot of teeth and can really slash his way through a school of minnows.

"Now, these dreams indicated that I had to control, to moderate my aggressiveness. But the water in these dreams was clearer than it had formerly been. So this was a hopeful sign. I was making spiritual progress.

"Lately, I've been fishing in clear water and I don't need any instrument. The water is in placid pools and I just stick out my hand and the fish come to me.

"The fish in these recent dreams are beautiful. They look to me like whitefish, or what you might call bluefish. They are whitish blue, almost silvery, and they sparkle when the sunlight hits them. And the water is crystal clear and I can see the fish swimming at all different depths.

"In the most recent dream I had of this nature, there were a bunch of people behind me and the fish were swimming to me and I was giving each person a fish. Now, I think this dream shows what I would like to overcome. I would like to quit giving people fish. That's what I'm doing when I give someone a reading; I'm giving him a fish. And what I would really like to do is to teach people how to *fish for themselves*.

"Which brings me back to the point: How to develop your own psychic powers.

"A question someone may well be thinking at this point is: How can I tell precisely which area of my life a particular dream refers to? How do I know when a dream reflects a physical problem—and it can—or a sexual problem, or has a spiritual meaning?

"One clue here is: What is of uppermost concern or interest in your mind at that particular time? If you have had reason to worry about your physical health, the dream well may pertain to that. If you're particularly concerned about money, your dream may shed light on that. If spiritual growth is uppermost in your mind, your dream likely will be about that.

"You'll develop an intuition as you go along as to which part of your life a particular dream pertains. You may be interested in three or four things at the same time. Then your dreams probably will reflect these in order of priority. The first dream you have during the night will refer to the problem you're *most* interested in; the second, to the next most important; and so on.

"Now, if you faithfully record your dreams and ponder them—you can ask for help in understanding a difficult dream during your meditation period, and this often works—whether you're making spiritual advances will become apparent to you through the dream symbolism. What will emerge in dream after dream is a pattern of similarities. In my case, climbing a hill meant getting higher spiritually. Others might dream they're flying and gradually they fly higher and higher. Others might be climbing steps and in successive dreams they get closer and closer to the top of the stairs.

"Now, let's go back to meditation. If you have real difficulty reaching the meditative level, there is a shortcut I recommend. Let me say, first, that some people have a terrible bugaboo about hypnosis. And I would agree that you should be very, very careful about whom you let hypnotize you. But if there is someone in whom you have confidence, go to him and say, 'Help me to achieve a state of hypnosis.'

"There is only one reason for you wanting to be hypnotized by someone else—to learn self-hypnosis faster. The easiest way to achieve a deep level of self-hypnosis is to be inducted into deep hypnosis by someone else and then have him switch control to you. This is done very simply. The hypnotist merely says, 'Whenever you wish to reach this deep level of consciousness on your own, you will simply take three deep breaths and repeat the word *peace* to yourself three times.' Or whatever. The point is that you can then quickly—in some cases, instantaneously—put *yourself* into a deep hypnotic or meditative state whenever you want to.

"Self-hypnosis is nothing more than an altered state of consciousness. But with it, you can achieve two things. First, if there's something you want to do or be—take off weight, improve your memory, overcome inferiority feelings—you can program yourself for this through self-hypnosis. Second, if you want to tap the deep levels of consciousness to gain inspiration and knowledge—from heaven knows where—I assure you, it will come. You go into the state of deep self-hypnosis, clear the mind completely, and you can ask and receive the answers to your problems.

"Now, you won't necessarily lose conscious awareness completely in the deep hypnotic state. I do, but that's because I patterned myself after Cayce and thought it was the only way. But it is *not* the only way.

"You can be in a state where you are halfway between consciousness and unconsciousness, and impressions will come to you. And you can speak these impressions as they come to you. They will just flow into your mind.

"Now, an advantage of this method is that you don't need a conductor. You can do it all yourself.

"To attain trance—the state of profound unconsciousness that I go into—is not necessary for the average person. You can get all the inspiration and psychic flashes you need in the half-conscious state, or what I call *reverie*. A reverie is simply a waking dream. And if you practice self-hypnosis long enough I guarantee that you will touch upon reverie. And what exactly is it like to experience reverie?

"Well, you will feel your whole being filled with such a warmth of pure love that if someone were to spit in your face and kick you in the ankle, you would continue to feel that love. You don't hate anybody or anything.

"Let me describe it this way: If you can imagine that

you're walking down the middle of a muddy road, wading in muck up to your knees, and you're as naked as a jaybird and a cold snow is blowing and there are people lined up on both sides pelting you with sharp stones, and yet you feel wonderful, loving, beyond caring what anyone does to you—then you have experienced reverie.

"You are still conscious; you know that your surroundings are there. But they've receded, they're unimportant to you. A sense of bliss and well-being envelops you.

"In addition, psychic impressions come in the reverie state. Spiritual impressions come. Insights into yourself and other people. What am I? What should I do with my life? These questions are answered in reverie.

"You can try out your psychic sensitivity by focusing on situations or individuals where strong emotion is involved. I think that's one reason why people can become very accurate in the psychic diagnosis of disease—because we get *damned* emotional about our own kidney stones, or an ulcer, or a palpitating heart, or partial blindness.

"So pick out something that has a *strong* emotional content for you to test your psychic powers. Ask a question that *means* something to you. Because ESP, other researchers have confirmed, seems to be facilitated or turned on by powerful emotion.

"A good place to start would be to try to tune in on your Aunt Bessie, whom you love, and do a physical checkup of her. You might get flashes in different ways. You might see her body with an X on it, a dark spot, meaning a problem in that area of the body. Or you might *feel* a pain in your chest, indicating that she has chest problems. You might just pick up the word 'pancreas,' and sense that something is wrong there. Psychic impressions come in different forms.

"Now, don't be discouraged, if at first you are less than 100 per cent accurate. I said at the outset that the growth of psychic powers is just *that*—growth—and it takes time.

"Learning to develop your psychic ability is no different really from learning to be an accountant, a truck driver, a good politician, a skilled physician. It takes practice. No one would ask you to teach physics if you had never learned physics. But you can go to school and learn physics and become accomplished enough to teach it. Yet even then, you won't know *everything* there is to know about physics; you won't be infallible on the subject. And the same is true in developing your psychic powers. They will gradually become more reliable, more accurate, but 100 per cent accuracy is unknown. Even Cayce had his off days. Certainly I do. The reason is that we're human and the psychic impressions are filtered through our human minds, which are often affected by the mood of the moment, the stresses we've been under, our physical state, what we've eaten and many other factors.

"Now, here is something I feel can't be stressed enough: Unless you are willing to develop spiritually and eliminate the defects in your personality as you develop your psychic powers, you'll become much more psychotic than psychic. You'll have many more disruptions in your life. You won't have the maturity to handle your psychic powers. You'll become what I call a 'flake.'

"You'll become an abnormal psychic, of whom there are many. And they live terrible lives. Others they help but themselves they cannot help. They are vexed by alcoholism, drug problems, emotional instability. The reason is that their psychic development has outstripped their spiritual development. They're psychic giants but spiritual pygmies.

"This would be like developing your hands to the exclusion of the rest of your body until you had grotesquely enlarged hands. Who wants that? The idea is to develop the whole you. If you neglect the spiritual and moral growth, you'll be out of whack, out of proportion.

"So the process of psychic development should not be

hurried. From the time you start until you begin getting consistent psychic results would probably take three and a half years, on the average. That's why you need patience and perseverance.

"Now, you'll have periods before then when you are almost 100 per cent on. However, these will be interspersed with setbacks. But gradually the setbacks will become fewer and the hits will become steady and consistent.

"Now, for the relatively lazy person, there's still hope for learning meditation if you utilize two periods which are natural for meditating: just before you fall asleep at night and just after you awaken in the morning.

"At these times, you are in what is called a hypnagogic state and the mind is very receptive to suggestions. I utilize these periods quite often for problem solving. I simply lie there in bed, either just before dropping asleep or immediately after awakening, and I put to myself about six times the question that's bothering me. Then the solution to the problem seems to come. I don't care whether it's a physical, financial or spiritual problem. The answer comes. Try it for yourself."

Ross Peterson also suggests that in the meditative, or hypnotic, or reverie state, whichever you call it, the subject ask for help or guidance from his "guides" or "angels."

"I definitely believe in angels," Peterson said, "and I think I've got nine who help me anytime I ask. If I quiet my mind and mentally ask them to help me, a form of communication takes place that is almost like talking to myself. But answers come which are wiser than I probably could ever come up with in my conscious state. If I follow the advice I receive at such times, it invariably works out beneficially for everyone. If I let my own ego get in the way and say, 'To hell with it, I ain't doing that,' I get into trouble. Deeper and deeper trouble, usually. It's like telling one lie, you know; you have to tell three more to cover up for it. So I have learned to follow the advice I receive. And at times I definitely feel that the advice represents guidance from my angels.

"Now, if you will try this for yourself—mentally ask your guides or angels to help you, or to make themselves known to you—sooner or later you will have the manifestation you ask for. You may see them while in meditation. Or you may feel a benevolent presence, or a group of such presences, surrounding you. Learn to ask help from your guides, for you *do* have them, and you'll receive help."

Ross Peterson said that there is one advantage of the deep trance state, the unconscious state which he achieves in his readings, over the reverie or half-conscious state.

"You can get more detail in the trance state. No doubt about it. If you want to actually climb inside someone's physical body and inspect it, organ by organ, the trance state seems necessary.

"If you want to go deeper than reverie then, into the very depths of your consciousness, so that you speak automatically, with no effort at all, and the words pour out of you, special measures must be followed.

"Ideally, you should find a teacher, someone who does it, to take you 'over the deep end,' into trance. But I'll tell you exactly how I enter the deep trance state, and if you want to make the plunge on your own, go to it.

"However, it won't be on your own. You need a conductor, someone with whom you are in harmony and who is willing to be very patient. What you look for in a conductor is someone who sincerely is empathetic with other people; who is kind, loving, giving and hopefully forgiving. Someone who is not a judgmental type. Because if you have someone who is out of tune with you, it's going to disturb the psychic results.

"Also, you should work with the same conductor for the best results. If you change conductors, it's like trying to learn physics with a series of different teachers, each picking up where the other left off.

"For a trance psychic to work with a conductor is a team effort. It takes time to build mutual confidence and trust.

"Well, let's assume that you've practiced meditation and gotten into a fairly deep state of self-hypnosis in which psychic flashes have been coming fairly consistently. How do you now go deeper?

"Here is exactly what I do.

"I loosen all my tight clothing. I take off my shoes. I loosen the neck especially. I always have a tendency to rub my eyes and forehead. I don't know if there is any physical reason for it but I feel comfortable doing that.

"Then I simply do a bit of deep breathing through the nostrils—three breaths on one side and three breaths on the other, inhaling into each nostril and exhaling through the mouth. The reason I do that is because a reading said to do it.

"Then I relax the body completely, starting with the top of my head and going to the toes. I've gotten to the point where I can do this in a minute or less. In the beginning it takes longer.

"Then I simply wait for the formation of that embryo pattern on my inner vision.

"Now, you probably won't see exactly what I see. Some people, at this stage, see blips of light, like many quivering stars. Some people see wavy lines across their inner field of vision. Some see colors, some see only black and white.

"Anyway, when I see my bluish embryo formation—and you will see your own individual symbol, maybe a star rising—then I know it's all right for me to go ahead. I say my prayer, 'Dear Lord, please help me to help these people.'

"The next thing I see is the faces of my angels or guides moving toward me in a semicircle, growing bigger as they come closer. Now, you may or may not experience this. I'm inclined to think that you will see it, or something comparable. I say that because it was quite spontaneous with me. I had no preconceptions or expectations which led me to look for this sort of thing. It just happened. And it will probably happen to you, though no doubt not in exactly the same way.

"When I see my guides, and feel love emanating from them—it's a feeling of great security—I begin a series of ten very deep abdominal breaths, counting to myself and beginning with ten and working downward . . . nine . . . eight . . . seven and so on.

"Now, just before I start counting I forcibly extend the diaphragm to take a very deep abdominal breath. And this is the signal for Irva, my conductor. And it can be the signal for your conductor.

"At this point, Irva begins counting with each breath I take. When I reach ten, she says the words 'Please clear the mind . . . and notify us when it is clear.'

"Usually I don't hear these words. When I begin counting my deep breaths, and I say, 'ten,' this sinking feeling begins. It's like fainting, if you've ever fainted, or being put out with an anesthetic like sodium pentothal.

"I count 'nine' and the swooning sensation gets stronger. Usually by the time I get to 'seven' or 'six' it happens. . . . I just drop into a deep unconscious state.

"Then, though I'm not aware of it, I respond to the conductor by saying, 'The mind is clear,' and Irva then gives me the instructions as to where, when, and to whom or to what my mind should go.

"When I first started, I often remembered my counting all the way down from ten to one. And sometimes I'd go under and get something, sometimes I wouldn't.

"Don't be discouraged if you successfully go under one day and then the next three attempts draw blanks. Keep at it. And eventually it will become totally consistent.

"If there is any state of mind that is conducive to going completely under I would have to call it an attitude of total surrender. You just trust God, your spirit guides, and your conductor and let go . . . completely.

"The next thing you know you'll be waking up from the trance and you won't be able to believe that you've actually been unconscious for an hour. And then when you hear a playback of the tape, and your own voice, yet not yours, droning on about things totally beyond your conscious knowledge—well, that's a mind-blowing experience, really."

Ross Peterson reiterated what he considers a *vitally* important part of embarking on a program of psychic development.

"Develop the whole person. In order to do this, first of all there must be some way by which you can achieve self-understanding. *Know thyself* is the key.

"Personally I found graphoanalysis extremely helpful in allowing me to see myself as I really was. Others have found a similar source of self-knowledge in astrology, or in a period of psychoanalysis with the right analyst. But I stress that knowing yourself, and having the courage to eliminate the defects from your character as you come to see them, is absolutely basic to real psychic development."

The steps he has outlined here, concluded Ross Peterson, provide enough guidance that if diligently followed anyone can expect to experience expanded awareness, increased God-awareness, and psychic functioning.

"Remember," he says, "they told me I was the most unpsychic person they had ever tested. If I did it, then anybody has the chance.

"Truly, I believe that being psychic is as natural as breathing and learning the skill is everyone's birthright . . ."

Because of the number of requests he has received from serious-minded seekers after expansion of consciousness, Ross Peterson has opened a retreat center where he is able to accommodate and train limited numbers of students.

He calls his center, Michigan Omnistic Research and Enlightenment, or MORE.

For information on the courses offered, write to:

Ross Peterson
Michigan Omnistic Research and Enlightenment
Laughing Gull Point
Garden, Michigan 49835